Watching the Thais

by

Tom Tuohy

Published in the UK in 2012 by Feed-A-Read.com

Copyright © Text Tom Tuohy

First Edition

ISBN 978 178 17666 9 9

Published in Thailand

What others say

"The writing is very literate. Tom Tuohy brings together a lot of information from various sources and puts it together to create a very useful orientation to Thailand." (Willam Page, author of *The Nirvana Experiments and Other Tales of Asia* and *Thai Lite*)

"Watching the Thais is as entertaining as it is informative. At times this book is laugh-aloud funny. A great read - informative and entertaining." (James Newman - Author of *Bangkok Express*.)

"Whether you're in Thailand for only a few days, or planning a longer stay, Tom Tuohy's book will give you a unique insight into the way Thais think, learn, walk, talk, shop, laugh, and love." (Merlin Lockey, author of *Death in Holy Orders*)"

Acknowledgments

This project would not have been possible without the support of many people. Many thanks must go to colleagues in Thailand, both Thai and western, and the many students I have taught there (especially from Pre-College, Mahidol University, and Chulalongkorn University's Continuing Education Centre), and also in the UK (The University of East Anglia and The University of Birmingham)

Also, thanks to those who explicitly gave permission to quote from their sources (web pages, books, journals, newspapers and magazines) and to those who voiced no objection. I would especially like to thank the following for their kindness in allowing me to quote from their own works: Michael P. Seaberg, Glenn Slayden, Kristian Gotthelf, Philip Roeland, Jennifer Gampell, Fran Woods, Piset Wattanavitukul, and Dennis Coday.

Special thanks must go to my long time friend, colleague, and confidante, Dr. Wannasin-Bell formerly at Thammasat University, without whom my knowledge of this beautiful country would have been greatly reduced. And finally, thanks to the numerous friends who endured this long process with me, always offering support and guidance.

Dedication

To my wife, Kornkaew, for her enduring patience.

'Your gaze scans the street as if they were written pages: the city says everything you must think, makes you repeat her discourse, and while you believe you are visiting Tamara you are only recording the names with which she defines herself and all her parts…However the city may really be, beneath this thick coating of signs, whatever it may contain or conceal, you leave Tamara without having discovered it. Outside the land stretches empty to the horizon; the sky opens, with speeding clouds. In the shape that chance and wind give the clouds you are already intent on recognizing figures: a sailing ship, a hand, an elephant…' (Italo Calvino *'Invisible Cities'*.)

'A problem cannot be solved at the same level of thinking in which it was created.' (Albert Einstein)

"To awaken quite alone in a strange town is one of the pleasantest sensations in the world." (Freya Stark)

Contents

Introduction

It has been said that each journey of a thousand miles begins with one small step. This book is a collection of many such small steps: a collection of essays and blogs reflecting my last fifteen years in Thailand. Seen in this light, each essay or blog post in this book represents some experience that I have had within my stay here in the kingdom, and tries to show some aspect of Thailand and its people to both the recent visitor and long term resident.

This book is neither long, nor is it meant as a self-help book: too many of them have already been published here in Thailand. My intention has been to steer clear of the style in which many books about visiting new cultures are written; ones which make obviously commonplace statements like 'X country is beautiful for Y reason', or 'X is full of friendly people for Z reason', or 'X country is simply X' (where the X factor is some ethereal entity that is simply not questioned further). The fact of the matter is that no country is perfect, not my own, and not any other, but sometimes it is the imperfection of something that also becomes part of its charm, part of its virtue and enchantment, and goes a long way in explaining why hundreds of thousands if not millions of visitors flock to its shores every year.

What this book is, is a book filled with a mixture of opinions, facts, anecdotes, lived experiences, and a host of other things, some complimentary to Thai culture and some less so. It is written with an insider's knowledge, but from an outsider's perspective. However, I would like to make it clear at the outset, that it is not my intention to show Thai people in a negative light, but rather to show them in a way that reflects their true nature; something that requires a certain degree of critical distance if a western audience is to genuinely better appreciate them as a race of people. If I have failed to achieve this in parts, I apologise to all Thai people in advance for the faults in my writing because I greatly admire their spirit and ingenuity, and love living in their beautiful country.

Indeed, I am painfully aware that any analysis of all things Thailand by me is bound to be wholly subjective and based merely on something I had read, heard about, or simply perceived as true and *not*, as in the case of the rest of the book, based on lived experience. This has been my guide throughout the writing of this book: to comment on something that, wherever possible, directly affected me personally.

I should also point out, however, that, where I offer my own opinion on Thai ways, or Thai life in general, I can promise that, at all junctures, I have made every effort to give my opinion in such a way that is not directly offensive to Thailand, its people, or its culture. I know that Thai people have a wonderful propensity for forgiveness, and if I have said something that upsets my gracious hosts, then I entreat, in advance, their forgiveness.

My principal reason for writing this book is to show that Thailand is a unique place to live in, replete with a magical language and genuinely warm-hearted people. Moreover, Thailand also has a truly amazing abundance of interesting attractions e.g. the food, the beaches, the wonderful climate, the beautiful women, the easy relaxed nature of its people. Indeed, I believe that Bangkok is as cosmopolitan as any Asian city, and is fast becoming a major hub in Asia, especially for my own passion, the Arts, entertainment in general, and especially its nightlife, its cuisine, and its blossoming fashion industry.

Yet, at the same time, I am also aware too that no culture is perfect whatever it's obvious or apparent virtues, and this is also an aspect that I believe the visitor should be aware of when visiting this beautiful country. In fact, because Thailand was never formally colonised by outside forces, it has, in some sense, its own particular way of doing things, peculiar talents that are home-grown because they have evolved exclusively within the context of a Thai landscape, among its people, and therefore cannot be found anywhere else. It is in this overarching context that I hope the reader will be able to form his or her own conception of what Thai people are, what the culture is all about, and how he or she might better understand the customs in this unique place.

I believe it was Charles Darwin who first discovered then formulated his theories based on the observation that certain species of animal (turtles if I'm not mistaken) were unique to the Galapagos Islands, varieties that could be found nowhere else on earth. I feel that in many ways, Thailand can be thought of and understood in such a light, with its specific mores and social customs. Thai culture is truly unique enough to lure, not only the ambitious botanist, but also the curious visitor and the enchanted tourist, indeed anyone who has the taste for a captivating experience, and who is open-minded enough to enjoy it. There really is something for everyone here, of all ages, races, and creeds; something that awaits those who are prepared to take that first step on a long journey into a strange, yet fascinating and magical land; into a culture that is steeped in history and tradition. Are you ready for that first step?

T.T.

(A smiling ticket collector does the rounds on the Chao Phraya River
Express Boat.)

Chapter One

The Thai Smile

The Cheshire Cats

"You're Never Fully Dressed without a Smile"

(From the musical, *Annie*)

'**Y**ou'd have to go a long way to find a nicer, friendlier bunch of people as the Thais', said the man in the job agency in Golder's Green London. My interview was for a teaching job in Thailand. Other than the few months I'd spent in Africa a few months earlier, I had no real experience of a classroom nor of teaching in another country, so this was going to be a real challenge. 'Just smile', he continued 'and everything will be fine!' At the time, I was struck with the simplicity of his advice, but, eight years later, I have come to see that that was the best advice anyone could've give me at the time.

As I have since learnt, Thais famously appear before you with grins larger than a Cheshire Cat's, and with a general demeanor that says 'I want to be your friend'. What is it about Thais that makes them so endearing through their smiles? How is it that this has become a national characteristic? I once read that an early meaning of the word 'Thai' also meant friendship, and it is fair to say that, as a race of people to the outsider, that is just how they appear - friendly, open people who desperately want to know and please you. However, this can be quite disarming at times, and these 'Thai smiles' are often the source of so much confusion when there is interaction between Thais and foreigners (farangs). This book aims to address some of these misconceptions.

Or is it simply a logical realization and acceptance that, when you smile at people, they tend naturally to treat you better? I remembered reading something the noted anthropologist Desmond Morris said,

'We smile in sympathy, in greeting, in apology, and in appreciation. It is without doubt the most important social bonding signal in the human gestural repertoire.' [1]

I wasn't sure what to think. Was a smile *really* the difference between being accepted in this culture or not? I decided to test my theory. When I had done all the necessary paperwork at my new job, signed what seemed like a million forms and registration documents, shook hands and greeted so many new faces, I headed for the nearby hotel recommended by the training manager.

The smile that greeted the receptionist at the hotel at the *Muang Phol* building could not have been beaming more broadly. Perhaps she thought I was some kind of eccentric because my smile could have cracked open a bottle of beer at twenty paces! All my less than pristine teeth and facial lines were positively straining to the maximum as they greeted the clearly perplexed receptionist. Not surprisingly, the room key was politely handed over, at arm's length, not unlike a scene from Faulty Towers, in an uncertain and slightly suspicious manner. I went to take a shower in my room upstairs, the receptionist's gaze following my every move as I made my way to the elevator. 'Ok, maybe I should lay off the smiles a little bit', I said to myself.

In their book, *Working with the Thais,* Henry Holmes and Suchada Tangtongtavy identify thirteen types of Thai smile, each with their own facial expression and corresponding meaning. They are called, 'A Baker's Dozen'.

1. *Yim thang taa*: The 'I'm-so-happy-I'm-crying' smile.

2. *Yim thak thaai*: The polite smile for someone you barely know.

3. *Yim cheun chom*: The 'I-admire-you' smile.

4. *Feun Yim*: The stiff smile, also known as the 'I-should-laugh-at-the-joke-though-it's-not- funny' smile.

5. *Yim mee lessanai*: The smile that masks something wicked in your mind.

6. *Yin yaw*: The teasing, or 'I-told-you-so' smile.

15

7. **Yim yae-yae**: The 'I-know-things-look-pretty-bad-but-there's-no-point-in-crying-over-spilt- milk' smile.

8. **Yim sao**: The sad smile.

9. **Yim haeng**: The dry smile, also known as the 'I-know-I-owe-you-the-money-but-I-don't- have-it' smile.

10. **Yim thak thaan**: The 'I-disagree-with-you' smile, also known as the 'You-can-go-ahead-and- propose-it-but-your-idea's-no-good' smile.

11. **Yim cheua cheuan**: The 'I-am-the-winner' smile, the smile given to a losing competitor.

12. **Yim soo**: The 'smile-in-the-face-of-an-impossible-struggle' smile.

13. **Yim mai awk**: The 'I'm trying-to-smile-but-can't' smile. [2]

It's no surprise that Thais have a classifying phrase for every smile because, as I shall show later, the structure of Thai society is very ordered and hierarchical. Just as Eskimos have twenty-six words for snow, so Thais have a non-verbal system for expressing themselves in a non-confrontational way. The Thai smile can therefore mean many different things depending on the context and individual situation, and the main confusion or misunderstanding arises when visitors to Thailand are simply not aware of that fact. As Jane Cafarella says in her 'Thai Diary',

> 'They [Thai people] smile happily, apologetically,
> hopelessly, nervously, just to name a few. You
> interpret the smile the same way someone reads
> a book - its meaning comes from the context.' [3]

Part of the reason why Thais have this outward display of inward feelings may be found in the very Thai idea of avoiding confrontation. There can be nothing more anathema to a Thai than to allow themselves to get angry or feel that he or she has caused another person to have a negative emotion. Thais, therefore, go out of their way to avoid situations, which may cause such results and, instead, wrap their feelings and anxieties up in smiles that are often quite disarming.

16

Khun Suriluck, a cross-cultural trainer and local teacher, explains that the Thais smile in almost every situation. 'Generally, the smile is to extend friendship and to welcome, but it can also mean 'I'm sorry or I don't know, or tough luck,' she says in her handbook. [4]

Another aspect of Thai culture that visitors either overlook, or simply don't fully understand, is the idea of 'losing face'. To cause someone to lose face is simply not done in Thai society and indeed any *faux pas* that surfaces, is simply accepted as an instance of human frailty and to be accepted as that, nothing more. Indeed, in Thai society, every caution is taken to ensure that nobody is made to feel bad or uncomfortable regardless of whether they made a mistake or brought disapprobation upon themselves. Thai people even have a phrase for it, 'Sabaii Sabaii' or, 'feel comfortable and relaxed'. From the lowliest or most humble motorcycle taxi driver to the boss of a large company, there is no qualitative difference in behaviour when a mistake is made. Allowances will be made and smiles will be shared all round for any folly that befalls either employee. Smiling is in fact the social glue that keeps everyone calm and polite. As Jane Cafarella says when trying to explain this,

> 'Losing face is taboo in Thai culture which makes
> it hard to tell someone when they've stuffed up
> [made a mistake]. Khun Siriluck had explained that
> most people cannot take direct comments or
> suggestions from their boss, so you had to skirt
> around it.' [5]

Thais have a deep sense of themselves as at all times being worthy of mutual respect and courtesy. It is for this reason that they have inbuilt mechanisms that ensure a smooth, happy-go-lucky approach to daily affairs. Suntaree Komin explains this well,

> 'Since the "ego" of the Thai is so important, it naturally
> follows that the Thai have the "avoidance mechanism"
> to fend off unnecessary clashes. And this intricate
> mechanism is delicately and keenly observed by all
> parties involved in an interaction. It is only cases
> where indirect means are not used that interactions

will result in negative feelings and emotional
outburst if provoked in public.' [6]

Of equal importance to an understanding of the Thai way of behaving, is to compare it to the western model. People from the West usually smile for reasons that have little to do anything other than that they have seen or heard something funny or amusing. Thais, however, as we've seen, smile for a whole variety of reasons, and those uninitiated into Thai ways of thinking and acting can often misinterpret this.

Part of the problem for visitors is in getting theirs heads around the fact that someone is smiling in X situation, when they are used to understanding that X situation as calling for a serious 'face' or serious response in that particular situation. When they encounter the opposite, they are likely to question its validity. For example, imagine that the pressure's on at work, and your Thai colleague just smiles it away in a seemingly flippant manner, or when someone's just crashed into your car and greets you with a warm smile. If you're from the west, you have been accustomed to, even conditioned to reacting in a particular way. Indeed, you would almost certainly be expected to be at least a little bit, if not downright *angry* in such situations, even to the point where you might confront the individual responsible. But in Thailand, such a reaction would invoke a degree of horror and should therefore be avoided at all costs since it would create disharmony and cause ill feeling. As Thomas J. Knutson says, 'Overt displays of anger jeopardize social harmony in Thailand, and indicate ignorance, immaturity, and vulgarity.' [7]

Why should this be so? Part of the reason may lie in the fact that we westerners are brought up to believe that 'everything happens for a reason' and if something bad happens, then it's 'nothing to smile about' Moreover, we are taught that we should 'take it seriously' and not 'fool around'. However, in Thailand, the word 'serious' is a cognate word and almost always invites a negative idea to a Thai mind. 'Don't serious' is a common Thai epithet meaning 'lighten up. Our upbringing and education are therefore both obstacles to understanding the Thai preference for hiding these unfortunate events under a veil of smiles.

Kriengsak Niratpattanasai seems to understand this well,

'Another point is about Thais smiling. In your
country, people are more 'rational'. They are
supposed to have a reason to explain each
behavioral trait including a smile. But Thai
society puts much emphasis on relationships.
They are nice people, who always harmonise
with each other. They have their own reasons
to smile. They want to create a friendly
atmosphere in the workplace. In fact, you
should be happy when your staff members are
happy. They will be much more productive if
they have good emotions in the office.' [8]

How then can visitors to Thailand possibly hope to bridge this gap
between Thais and visitors to their country, especially long-term visitors?
Is it even possible for such visitors to fully understand them, given the
ambiguous way they smile, not only at us, but also at each other? In
'Customs & Etiquette: When in Thailand' we learn the full force of this
ambiguity,

'Thais are famous for their smiles. The Thai smile can
say many things. Thais smile when they are happy,
amused, embarrassed, uncertain, wrong, annoyed or
furious. As westerners, we are not generally able to
interpret the type of smile we are receiving but be
aware that it may *not* mean what you think it means.' [9]

This is an intriguing statement because for me it neatly sums up some
westerner's perception of Thais as 'shallow' or 'economical with the truth'
(if I may borrow a famous euphemism). But the fact of the matter is that
Thais feel that it is better to hide behind a smile or even tell a 'white lie' if
it means that a confrontation can be avoided, or that someone's 'blushes
might be spared'. Daniel Fraser illustrates this well,

'In Thailand smiling is a form of subtle interpersonal
-messaging which runs deeper and perhaps more
accurately than language or syntax. Investigation
into this phenomena reveals that Thais are adept at
performing no less than Thirteen situational-specific
smiles in their everyday lives. In fact, most Thais

19

can perform each smile upon request with flawless accuracy based solely on the commonly used name of each. In addition, Thais are experts at identifying the specific smiles they encounter, and are well aware of the inherent message behind each. Thirteen specific kinds of smiles? How could one possibly know the difference and know how to interpret each one? Many of the smiles that Thais perform are used to relieve tension, calm nerves, seek forgiveness or omission from distressing situations. The name of one particular smile, yim soo, translates as the 'smiling-in-the-face-of-an -impossible-struggle' smile. (above).' [10]

There are countless other situations where Thai people smile, for example, in adversity. The following example of this is perhaps most significant because it truly highlights the Thai personality. I'll let Bob Wilde explain,

'But the Thai smile, so famous to all visitors, is just a little more than a smile. It is often a sign of embarrassment, or distaste. In the 70s an Egyptian airline pilot mistook the lights of a factory for the runway and crashed on top of the factory. Many victims died a hideous death by burning. At such times of disaster, various groups – the Red Gaurs for example - are called in to take the bodies to morgues, and I well remember a picture in the Thai newspapers of a Thai carrying a body so hideously burnt that it had been reduced to half its normal size. The Thai carrying this horrifying object was smiling. But not from any sense of comedy; it was his natural facial reaction to horror.· [11]

We would normally call this 'putting on a brave face', and again as Jane Cafarella says, it is only the context that would tell other Thai people the feelings behind the smile. Actually, many people of all nationalities on the Thai beaches witnessed this particular smile after the Asian Tsunami of 2004 struck with such devastating results. But for all the ambiguity and uncertainty, each smile, whatever its origin, has its own story behind it.

I remember one such story an English training manager once told me, which perhaps best sums up the true value of a particularly communicative

Thai smile. He had been scheduled to meet a Thai manager to discuss a business English teaching course at the company. Unfortunately, nobody had agreed with the senior boss's idea of scrapping the said classes. When the training manager arrived he was seated, but a few minutes later the boss arrived and enquired as to why he [training manager] was there. The Thai lady who had set up the meeting smiled her broadest smile and simply told the boss that he was just there to have lunch. Satisfied with her answer, he promptly left.

A little stunned by the blatant lie, the English training manager gently asked later why she had lied to her boss. She explained that it was not unusual to do this in Thai society, as it was a case of 'what the boss doesn't see, can't hurt him'. In other words, she was trying to say that in some way she was protecting him by making sure that he was not aware of any irregularities that were taking place. If some should appear at a later date, he was covered under Thai etiquette because he was (truly) unaware of what was going on. A corporate case of 'ignorance is bliss'. She went on to explain that since Thais prefer to avoid confrontation, this was considered the proper thing to do as nobody would get hurt.

What is clear then is that given this understanding of Thai social interaction, westerners should always strive to understand that a smile *can* and often *does* mean a myriad of things, based on context, human relationship, proximity, etc., etc. We mustn't do what so many westerners do which is to don the negative cap of one particular smile, the *yim soo*, which, as we've seen translates as the 'smiling-in-the-face-of-an-impossible-struggle' smile, because our ability to integrate should never be seen in such a negative light. What is important is that we learn to recognize, like Thais do, *all* the smiles of the 'Baker's Dozen' and, as the old saying goes, when you find a chance to 'laugh...the whole world laughs with you!'

I'll let the Dalai Lama have the last word, for he is the person who best sums up the value of a smile,

> 'For me, human beings' ability to smile is one of
> our most beautiful characteristics. It is something
> no animal can do. Not dogs, nor even whales or
> dolphins, each of them very intelligent beings with
> a clear affinity for humans, can smile as we do.' [12]

21

And who could argue with that?

Chapter Notes:

[1] Morris, Desmond, *The Human Animal: A Personal View of the Human Species —The Language of the Body*, Journal of Linguistic Anthropology, June 2003, Vol. 13, No. 1: pp. 123-124.
http://www.anthrosource.net/doi/pdf/10.1525/jlin.2003.13.1.123

[2] Holmes, Henry and Tangtongtavy, Suchada, *Working with the Thais,* White Lotus Co., Limited, 1995. http://www.smilingalbino.com/stories/

[3] Cafarella, Jane, *Thai Diary: Digging Beneath the Surface*
http://www.abc.net.au/rn/talks/lm/stories/s1304563.htm

[4] Khun Suriluck (taken from Cafarella, Jane, *Thai Diary: Digging Beneath the Surface*)

[5] Op Cit, Cafarella, Jane

[6] Komin, Suntaree, NATIONAL CHARACTER IN THE THAI NINE VALUES
ORIENTATIONS, from *Psychology of the Thai People: Values and Behavioral Patterns*, National Institute of Development Administration (NIDA), (1991)
http://www.fulbrightthai.org/knowledge/read.asp?id=28&type=culture

[7] Knutson, Thomas J., *TALES OF THAILAND, LESSONS FROM THE LAND OF SMILE*,
http://www.fulbrightthai.org/knowledge/read.asp?id=27&type=culture

[8] Niratpattanasai, Kriengsak, '*Bridging the Gap, - Impressing the boss, alienating your colleagues*',
http://www.bangkokpost.net/090505_Business/09May2005_biz13.php

[9] *Customs & Etiquette: When in Thailand*
http://www.eslmonkeys.com/teacher/country_info/country.php?country=T
hailand&field=customs&title=Customs%20%26%20Etiquette

[10] Fraser, Daniel, '*Thai Smiles - Good, Bad, Ugly, and the 10 in
    between*'.
http://www.smilingalbino.com/stories/smiles.asp

[11] Wilde, Bob, *The Thai Smile*,
http://www.ethailand.com/index.php?id=768

[12] His Holiness The Dalai Lama, *Ethics For The New Millennium*,
Howard C. Cutler, M.D., Putnam Publishing Paperback, May 2001
    http://www.bookbrowse.com/excerpts/index.cfm?book_number=153

(A view of a tug boat and ferry passing under Pinklao bridge, Bangkok.)

Chapter Two

The Thai Social System

Collectivism versus Individualism

One of the first things that I noticed when I had not been long in Thailand was the way in which Thais like to do things in groups. In fact, the bigger the group, the better. It seemed at times like they were all 'joined at the hip' and incapable of doing anything alone. This struck me as I had been brought up in London where people do things in a ruthlessly individualistic fashion, and indeed to be different from the 'pack' or the 'herd' was a prized attribute. At the time, I wondered if this really was the Thai 'National Characteristic'.

However, once again this is a common misunderstanding that exists among visitors to Thailand. As I said before, Thai society is rigidly structured in a hierarchical way so that the group is the dominant force, not the individual members of which it is comprised. However, as I shall show, this allows a good deal of freedom of movement within its realm. As John Embree says in his exceptional essay, *Thailand a Loosely Structured Social System*, Thailand is also defined as 'loosely woven' as opposed to a 'tightly woven' culture, meaning '...a culture...here signifying [one] in which considerable variation in individual behaviour is sanctioned.' [1]

From every aspect of life, from eating, socializing, co-operating in a joint project at work, or attending social gatherings (weddings, funerals etc.) Thais will bond together and form a cohesive group. Yet, within that group, there is considerable scope for individualistic interpretation of what the right course of action should be in any given situation. This is as instinctual to Thais as ants working in colonies or bees making honey in hives. They do it automatically and seldom see the need to question why they do so.

And of course, this can be very frustrating for those who are not in any one of these particular social groups. As anyone who has had to deal with government departments (Immigration, Labour Dept. etc.) will tell you, trying to get the necessary papers, and on time, is often fraught with difficulty. Part of the reason for this is as I said not being in the 'group', but it is also because, as Holmes and Tangtontavy say in their *Working with the Thais*, '... Thailand ranks 41st, out of 53 cultures surveyed, indicating a strongly 'collectivist' society.' [2] It is this notion of collectivism that protects the individual by giving them a clearly defined role within the hierarchy. Harry C. Triandis, a famous psychologist had this to say on the subject,

> 'Collectivist societies put high value on self-discipline,
> accepting one's position in life, honouring parents and
> elders, and preserving one's public image for the sake of
> the group. While collectivists are very nice to those who
> are members of their own groups, they can be very nasty,
> competitive and uncooperative towards those who aren't.
> There is an unquestioned obedience in one's own group
> and even willingness to fight and die for it, and a distrust
> of those in other groups.' [3]

Moreover, as Holmes and Tangtontavy also tell us, Thais have three social circles in which they primarily move. They are called: (1) the family circle, (2) the cautious circle, and (3) the selfish circle. It is the last circle that visitors to Thailand often meet with when they are waiting for visas to be processed, have just been barged off the road by a four-wheel drive pick up, or served food in a restaurant *after* guests who arrived much later. Yes, of course this can be incredibly frustrating, but being armed with this knowledge may help you to be *jai yen* and keep your cool when all others around you may be losing theirs.

I remember an incident a few years ago in a French delicatessen called *Deli France* on Silom Road, Bangkok. An American woman had ordered a particular meal, cooked in exactly the way she liked it. I watched her give exact instructions to the waitress, even down to how the lettuce should be presented on the plate When the food didn't arrive on time, she created a fuss and asked, neigh *demanded* to see the manager. The manager, a bespectacled Thai thirty something lady, duly arrived and listened patiently to this obnoxious woman's tirade though eventually, through a mixture of smiles and diplomacy, managed to pacify her.

I watched the reactions of the staff and customers alike: it was one of extreme embarrassment on both sides. The Thais were embarrassed because of course they hate confrontations, especially where someone 'loses their cool', while the guests, who were mostly foreigners, were embarrassed and a little ashamed to be guests in Thailand.

It also reminded me of the old adage that 'People travel a thousand miles but never really leave home'. This woman obviously had an inflated sense of her own importance as an *individual* which had come to clash with the way things are done in a *collectivist* society. With delusions of grandeur, she had traveled thousands of miles from America expecting the same food, the same service, and general pandering to her whimsical needs. She had made a mistake that so many visitors to Thailand make: expecting everything to be the same as the place they just came from and finding they were wrong. A good lesson therefore for those intending to visit Thailand is to remember that things are done differently here and when for example things are done in a way you don't expect – your taxi is going a different way, your food is late, or you get something you didn't order, a big smile followed by a calm enquiry will almost always get you a more positive outcome.

Of course the case of the American lady is an extreme one, but it does highlight the expectations that people have when they visit a new country and have always had X done in X way, or Y done in Y way. When you have been brought up to believe that Z is true in all cases where Z occurs, you are often ill-equipped to deal with the situation that arises when you are presented with something else, as our American lady demonstrated.

However, while this may illustrate the Thai way of doing what's best for the group, it is also interesting to look at the apparent 'looseness' and relaxed interpretation of rules that exists in Thai culture. Although, as we've said, the concerns of the group take precedence over the individual in Thai society, nevertheless Thais display a remarkably individualist

28

character streak, too. Embree highlights many other contradictory elements of the Thai way of thinking of the group over the individual,

> 'The first characteristic of Thai culture to strike an
> observer from the west, or from Japan or Vietnam,
> is the individualistic behaviour of the people. The
> longer one resides in Thailand the more one is struck
> by the almost determined lack of regularity, discipline,
> and regimentation in Thai life. In contrast to Japan,
> Thailand lacks neatness and discipline; in contrast to
> Americans, the Thai lack respect for administrative
> regularity and have no industrial time sense.' [4]

This is something of an anomaly since on the one hand, as we've seen, Thai culture is very much ordered with a top down approach to all aspects of human interaction. Yet, at the same time, as we've seen from Embree, when questioning whether or not Thailand's loosely structured social system has survival value, comes to the realization that Thais can also be very slack in matters like time, personal responsibility, and the care and attention which they place on order and routine. At times it may appear as though the Thais want to obey the rules only if and when it suits them, but this is only because there is a greater degree of freedom in their culture to interpret the rules themselves.

Again, this is something that the visitor misunderstands by simply being unaware of the cultural mechanisms that give rise to and thus *underpin* Thai culture, per se. It is important to be aware then that, just because you are not in that particular social circle or group, does not necessarily mean that you are an enemy of that group, or that its members look on you unfavorably, rather like George Bush Junior's post 9/11 dictum – 'You are either with us, or against us'. This is how most visitors to Thailand interpret such situations, and is also where a lot of cross-cultural tension arises. Being outside of the circle does not automatically mean you are 'out of the loop'. It simply means that your relationship to the host culture is different.

Another aspect that underpins the Thai collectivist spirit and which Thais are proud of, is something that is often quoted in bars and restaurants from

29

Sukumvit to Silom. It is the fact that Thailand was never colonized while all its neighbours were. This is very important to the collective Thai psyche because it has emboldened them to see themselves as a strong and independent spirit - proud and unconquerable. As Embree says, the Thais were able to avoid colonization because they were able to utilize the same self-defense mechanism, which neutralizes situations when conflict arises in their own society. Suntaree Komin calls this the 'avoidance mechanism' or the 'uncertainly avoidance' principle,

> 'This third national culture attribute refers to the
> extent to which a society feels threatened by
> uncertain and ambiguous situations and tries to
> avoid them. A society of high uncertainly avoidance
> is characterized by a high level of anxiety among its
> people, which manifests itself in greater nervousness,
> stress, and aggressiveness. Because they feel
> threatened by uncertainly and ambiguity in the society,
> so, mechanisms are created to provide security and
> reduce risk.' [5]

I quoted earlier the situation with the English Training Manager (Chapter One) where the situation was resolved with a big smile and a lie. The same mechanism was, according to Embree, responsible for helping the Thais resist foreign occupation. In plain English, we might politely call this diplomacy, or more accurately, it allowed them to use doubletalk to keep their enemies in the dark, and thus, at bay,

> 'What saved it [Thailand] was the diplomatic skill
> of the Thai, a kind of delay and doubletalk, which
> doubtless irritated more than one foreign diplomat,
> but which succeeded in preventing them from ever
> joining forces to carve up the country.' [6]

It is this emphasis on dialogue that the Thai resorts to in times of tension which follows Winston Churchill's dictum that, 'It is better to jaw-jaw than to war-war!' [7] Again, Embree explains this well,

> 'In her diplomacy, Thailand succeeds in exploiting her
> cultural differences from the West. While never so

30

adamant in her resistance to some western demand as to force a showdown fight and sure defeat, what the Thai government official does is first to smile and if this is not sufficient to disarm the unwelcome stranger he also says, smilingly, 'Yes, I'll see'. In the weeks, months, or years of 'seeing' how the foreigner's wish can be implemented, some new factor enters the picture either to make the foreigner change his mind or to give the Thai government some opportunity backed by outside strength to give a negative reply'. [8]

This cultural *modus vivendi* contrasts starkly with Teddy Roosevelt's well-known proverb advising, as a brief statement of his approach to foreign policy, the tactic of caution and non-aggression, backed up by the ability to do violence if required.

'There is a homely old adage which runs: 'Speak softly and carry a big stick; you will go far.' If the American nation will speak softly, and yet build and keep at a pitch of the highest training a thoroughly efficient navy, the Munroe Doctrine will go far.' [9]

What I want to suggest therefore is that this is an important aspect of Thai culture – the ability to give relatively benign answers to seemingly difficult questions or requests, and at all costs to avoid a showdown. As we saw before with the example of the English Training Manager and the Thai employee, a certain doubletalk or diplomatic answer is very much something that is valued even prized within Thai culture because, as I said, the group's welfare is more important than any single member.

Embree characterizes this as the ability to tell a lie and, while doing so, to be *choei* (calm) whenever and wherever necessary. In other words, to be able to stay cool and collected in tense situations, like Castiglione 's [10] notion of sprezzatura or 'courage under fire', is the social exemplar to which all Thais aspire. It is this very same stillness and passivity, a certain disinterestedness, which Thais portray when they find themselves in problem situations, but which, nevertheless allows them to remain calm, and thus render them better able to defuse potentially volatile situations.

Moreover, as Embree suggests, Thailand managed, through lies and doubletalk, to retain political independence while all the small countries of the Southeast Asia succumbed to European control. He suggests that this was due to the combination of good luck and clever diplomacy. He believes that just being a geographic buffer could not in itself have saved Thailand. Thai diplomatic skill was key to maintaining autonomy. For Embree, as we've seen, Thai diplomacy is marked by delay and doubletalk and is a reflection of Thailand's loosely structured social system. For, in Thailand to tell a lie successfully or to dupe someone is praiseworthy. As Charles McHugh says, 'Thais go out of their way to maintain amicable relations with others and so they may even tell a small lie to prevent strained relations.' [11]

But of course we must, lest we wish to offend our hosts, be careful to distinguish between a lie for the sake of personal gain, which for the Christian would be a cardinal sin, and this kind of lie, the Thai lie. This kind of lie is more in keeping with the Christian 'white lie' variety because it is done either with the intention of placating someone, or for some other way of benefiting the group as a whole. This is more in keeping with Upton Sinclair's notion thus, 'It is difficult to get a man to understand something when his salary depends upon his not understanding it.' [12]

According to Embree, 'A good liar, of course, requires a cool temperament, and Thais accord considerable respect to this'.[13] Moreover, once again we must fully understand the positive function and application that this has within the collectivist notion of what it means to be Thai. K. Landon expresses this well,

> 'The word is seldom applied in a derogatory manner unless used
> by a foreigner who is trying to break lassitude and indifference.
> Siamese regard it as complimentary and the attitude that it expresses
> as a virtue. It means to ability to take life as it comes without
> excitement. He who meets the crises of life with cool mien is
> 'choei'. A certain girl, whoheld a prominent position and who, when
> caught in adultery and theft and stood to lose both good name and
> position, met the situation with a coolness that was most astonishing,
> and was described by Siamese as undeniably choei. The term implies
> coolness of attitude towards work, responsibility or trouble.' [14]

But of course, while Thais may aspire to this ideal of coolness, it is not always achieved. Occasionally, when Thais do lose their cool, things can become very heated indeed, and with deadly results. This is because for the Thais, the sense of self, the ego is elevated to a much higher degree. As Komin says,

> 'Thai people have a very big ego, a deep sense of independence, pride and dignity. They cannot tolerate any violation of the "ego "self. Despite the cool and calm front, they can be easily provoked to strong emotional reactions, if the "self' or anybody close to the "self" like one's father or mother, is insulted.' [15]

And when situations arise in public, this avoidance mechanism, which we talked about, is sometimes *not* utilized. Komin tells an interesting story to illustrate this,

> 'There are countless numbers of examples in the media, where people can readily injure or kill another person for seemingly trivial insults. Take for example, a party in which the host was celebrating his winning the black -market (*Huey tai din*), a guest (guest A) was getting impatient for the delayed local puppet show (*Nang talung*) and started making noises. Angry when he was reprimanded by another guest (guest B), he yelled at guest B to mind his own business. Apparently, guest B's big ego cannot take guest A's remark, he beat A's head with a whisky bottle, and gunned him down right between his eyes.' [16]

On a personal note, I remember a few years ago sitting at a table having a beer at one of those outside bars, which are ubiquitous in Bangkok. There was a boxing match (*Muay Thai*) being shown on a small TV in front of me, and a group of older Thai men were busy waving their fists in the air, shouting for their man and generally engaged in the usual effusive gestures of excitement that accompany local boxing matches. Two guys arrived on a motorbike and the owner of the bar approached one of them as he was getting off the bike. An argument ensued, presumably about an unpaid gambling debt connected to the boxing, or some other perceived insult, and an altercation resulted. The younger man punched the bar owner so cleanly that he ended up on the floor in a split second. What did the older man do? He got up, ran into his shop and returned a second or two later with a large machete.

What followed was something like a scene from the Keystone Cops, with the younger man running down the street, followed in hot pursuit by the machete-wielding bar owner. The two men then started running around one particular car - this way, that way - until finally the younger man began to *wai* the older man profusely. He did this by moving slowly towards his would-be attacker almost like a dog would edge closely to an aggressive rival, his hands close to his face as if praying. A brief conversation followed whereby the *wai* was returned by the older man and the problem, whatever it was, resolved. This is probably what Komin means when she says of the Thais,

> 'The popular phrase "*Kling wai korn, pho sorn wai*"
> (Do whatever is called for at the moment, to survive),
> perhaps adequately depicts the flexible characteristic
> of the Thai people.' [17]

But of course these are by and large isolated incidents and only serve to illustrate the extreme nature of the Thais when pushed towards anger. It does not in any way serve to illustrate the many acts of kindness to which the Thais are well known and indeed produce on a daily basis. This is merely one aspect of their psychology, which the visitor to Thailand must be aware of if they wish to maximize their stay in this beautiful kingdom. As we have said, once the Thais step out of their collectivist understanding through a perceived personal insult which hurts their ego, it would be unwise to do anything further to aggravate the situation. I'll leave Thomas J. Knutson to have the last word on the real Thai spirit,

> 'Thais are nice people. Other countries of the world
> may excel in economic power, military strength, and
> technological ability, but Thailand surely leads the
> world psychologically. The gentleness and genuine
> charm of the Thai people serve as a model for the
> enjoyment of diversity and the acceptance of
> differences.' [18]

Chapter Notes:

[1] Embree, John F, *Thailand A Loosely Structured Social System*, American Anthropologist, April- June, (1950) Vol.52 (2):181-193. http://www.publicanthropology.org/Archive/Aa1950.htm

[2] Holmes, Henry and Tangtontavy, Suchada, *Working with the Thais*, White Lotus Co., Limited, (1995). http://www.smilingalbino.com/stories/

[3] Triandis, Harry C., *Individualism versus Collectivism*, Westview Press, (1995).http://www.getcited.org/GuestScreen?PUBLICATION_ID=10128 9361&PUBLISHER_NAME=Greenwood+Press&x=7&y=2

[4] Op Cit., Embree, J.F.

[5] Komin, Suntaree, Psychology of the Thai People: Values and Behavioral Patterns (1990) in NATIONAL CHARACTER IN THE THAI NINE VALUES ORIENTATIONS.

[6] Op Cit, Embree, J.F.

[7] Churchill, Winston, (remarks at a White House luncheon, June 26, (1954). His exact words are not known because the meetings and the luncheon that day were closed to reporters, but above is the commonly cited version.)

[8] Op Cit, Embree, J.F.

[9] Roosevelt, Theodore, American president, speech in Chicago in April, (1903) http://www.bartleby.com/59/12/speaksoftlya.html

[10] Baldassare, Castiglione, Italian diplomat and author, wrote the *Book of the Courtier,* in which   the term sprezzatura was coined. It described the art of making the difficult seem effortless.

[11] McHugh, Charles, J.F., *Reaction Profiles by Americans, Chinese, Japanese, Thai, and Vietnamese on 'Skeletons in the Family Closet'*, Setsunan University, Osaka, Japan.
http://www.immi.se/intercultural/nr1/McHugh.htm

[12] Sinclair, Upton, *I, Candidate for Governor: And How I Got Licked* (1935) http://en.wikiquote.org/wiki/Upton_Sinclair

[13] Op Cit, McHugh, Charles, J.F.

[14] Landon, K., *Siam in Transition*, Chicago, (1939).
http://www.publicanthropology.org/Archive/

[15] Op Cit, Komin, S, (1990)

[16] Ibid, Komin, S. (1990)

[17] Ibid, Komin, S. (1990)

[18] Knutson, Thomas J., *TALES OF THAILAND, LESSONS FROM THE LAND OF SMILE*
http://www.fulbrightthai.org/knowledge/read.asp?id=27&type=culture

(Two unusually dressed foreigners walking off the boat at a pier in Bangkok)

Chapter Three

Thais and Movement

Keep on Walking, Johnny Walker

Watch any Thai walking down the street and you will soon discover something interesting about their general gait. This is because Thais are not given to walk with any great assurance that they have a definite destination in mind. There's no Johnny Walker peering back at you with a walking stick, Chaplin-like, and a cheerful smile. On the contrary, the visitor to Thailand could be forgiven form assuming that the Thai penchant for walking was in point of fact *non-existent*.

The fact of the matter is that Thais abhor walking almost as much as they detest hot weather. A common source of moans heard from Thais is to do with the weather – '*lorn mahk*', means 'it's very hot' or '*agaat mai dee*' means 'the weather's bad'. These are regular utterances of Thai people on an almost daily basis. And if you're a long time resident, you'll come to the conclusion that the all-year-round tropical heat has rendered the Thais unwilling even to walk the shortest distance in their own city, especially during the working day. As Philip Roeland explains,

> 'Thais aren't particularly good at walking. By walking,
> I mean just walking around in the shopping mall, on
> the pavement, anywhere really. I don't refer to hiking
> or trekking; those activities are entirely foreign to most
> Thais. People who do that are completely out of their
> mind, if you'd ask Somchai Samsong (the average
> Thai, in analogy with Joe Sixpack). No, I'm talking
> about using your feet to get from one place to another
> in daily situations.' [1]

Actually, Roeland is wrong about one thing - Thais love nothing more than to wander around malls and stores; shopping is in fact a national pastime (as you'll see in Chapter Seven). It's an activity that most Thai people relish and spend a great deal of time doing. This is partly because malls and shopping centers are always very cool and fully air-conditioned. It's also because shopping is a way that Thai people show that they care about others because they really enjoy giving gifts to their family and friends.

However, Roeland's main point about Thais hating to walk to actually *get somewhere* is correct. Part of the reason for this is that Thai streets are not the most inviting and user-friendly. In fact they are often a hazard to your health with a host of obstacles that have to be overcome on a daily basis, as Bangkok Bob explains,

> 'There are several ways to get about Bangkok, although the most obvious one, WALKING, is the least practical as Bangkok is hardly pedestrian friendly. The pavements are a place where you have to compete for space with motorcycles, parked cars, street vendors, street restaurants, barbecues, vats of boiling oil, and various strange objects left lying around from recent construction projects. Not to mention holes, broken – missing or damaged inspection covers, water pipes, water meters, and cables, it has to be seen to be believed!' [2]

Another reason is that walking outside, for example, during your lunch break to find the nearest MacDonald's or delicatessen will ensure that you look like a sun-drenched pizza delivery boy upon your return to the office. Then you'll have your Thai colleagues looking at you in a seemingly nonchalant way as if to say 'should've ordered in!'

Now, let's *not* get into thinking that there's something wrong with the way Thais walk. Let me repeat that – THERE'S NOTHING WRONG WITH THE WAY THAI PEOPLE WALK! It's just that they, you know, they…walk…kinda …slowly. I remember walking down the street in Siam Square when I first arrived in 1997. It was the time when I still walked like a foreigner – quickly. I have since learnt to walk like a Thai person – slowly. It was the soi around the corner from the Lido Cinema.

It's famous for it's rickety pavements, and you have to be on your guard when you trod that route lest you wish to disappear through the cracks, break your ankle, and never be seen again like something from that movie *Being John Malkovich*!

On this occasion I was late for a class just around the corner and was belting at great speed dodging in and out of the groups of young people, mostly teens, who were ambling aimlessly in front of me. Then I came upon a large group of teens walking together. I tried to get past one way, but that way was blocked. Then I tried the other, but there were too many cars in the way to sort of squeeze my portly frame through any indiscernible gap. Finally, I just waded through the group apologizing profusely as I went. The looks I got ranged from total disbelief, to well...total disbelief actually. A Thai would never be so rude as to simply brush past people like that, and not for the first time I benefited from being a foreigner in the sense that no harm came to me. Roeland continues,

> 'What's wrong with the way Thai people walk? Objectively speaking, probably nothing. As always, experiencing another culture involves comparison with your native culture, however objective you try to be. I'd say that my normal walking pace is about twice that of the locals. This means that, according to my view of the world, Thais walk incredibly slowly.' [3]

I concur. Another facet of Thai perambulations is the way Thai people cross the street. Thais will invariably try to cross highways, usually in groups, but with scant regard for each other's safety. A common thing that I see is a Thai person simply walking between cars to cross the street with barely a glance at the oncoming traffic. It sometimes seems like they have a death wish, the lack of circumspection and general wariness they show in some traffic situations. Actually I later came to realize that Thai drivers won't give way to let you cross the road *unless* you actually step onto it and start walking. This is the sign that you *really* do want to cross. Again Roeland explains it this way,

> 'I do like a leisurely stroll in the park myself occasionally, but I'd never dream of obstructing pedestrian traffic wherever I go the way Thais do. I realise it's no big deal, but their perambulations sometimes get on my nerves. I guess they are so slow because they don't like to walk and they are

hardly ever in a hurry. The tropical heat, the culture at work or the lack of a job are probable causes.' [4]

Of course you have to ask how you yourself would respond in a climate that was hot all-year-round? Wouldn't you find some system that ensured you didn't have to spend too much time out in the heat? I sometimes joke with my students that there are three seasons in Thailand – hot, hotter, and the hottest. April in Thailand can, and often does, reach 40 degrees Celsius and above, with the result that five minutes out in that unforgiving sun is simply unbearable. It brings a whole new meaning to T S Eliot's idea that 'April is the cruelest month.' [5] But it does highlight an important cultural trait of the Thai people, one that benefits others as Roeland reminds us,

> 'Fortunately, there is an economic advantage to this aversion to walk. The fact that Thais are completely unwilling to do the tiniest bit of walking makes the day for all kinds of taxi services. Especially motorbike taxis which benefit from the Thai reluctance to walk even 200 metres (I am not exaggerating).' [6]

Another aspect that warrants attention is the way Thai people drive. Whether you are in a big city like Bangkok, or a smaller suburb, there isn't a whole lot of difference in the way people drive. At first I thought it was pure unadulterated recklessness. Then I realized that there was in fact a method to their apparent madness. Motorcycle taxi drivers drive in and out of traffic at breakneck speed with the grace and skills of a ballerina, yet clinging onto the back of a skidding motorcycle for dear life is *not* something I'd recommend on a hot, stuffy Tuesday afternoon. I have done it many times before the arrival of the Skytrain, on my way to teach corporate classes, and have had more brushes with seemingly imminent death than I care to remember. On such occasions, external wing mirrors were clipped so often, that they found their way regularly into my dreams, and I would wake up from my slumber in a cold sweat with visions of drivers or passengers opening their car door at the very last second as I was passing by, with the result that, in the dream, I would often wake up in a Thai hospital with the equivalent of Nurse Sunanta administering severe unction. As Stephen Cleary recommends in his funny *Do's & Don'ts....To Truly Unseen Thailand,*

> "Do take a motorbike-taxi ride, speeding through the traffic like a Loony Tunes character you'll be in for one darned… 'scary experience." [7]

Car drivers too, seem to have learnt their driving skills in the Barney Rubble School of Motoring. As Stephen continues,

> "Driving in Thailand is not easy, you need to be aware of what is happening all round the vehicle, and special care must be taken due to the practice of overtaking on the inside, although this is officially illegal, it is the norm." [8]

Indeed it is, and now there are even traffic ads on Thai TV warning Thai motorists not to weave in and out 'like a snake'. The imagery is quite appropriate, I think.

Tailgating is another of the more pernicious aspects of getting around in Thailand. When at the wheel, I have lost count of the number of times I have had to cross into other lanes to escape the Thai version of Evil Kaneval: Somchai the pick-up driver-cum-fruit-seller-cum-labourer who's on his way to fill in for his cousin, a doctor at Bumrungrad Hospital. It starts with a glance in your wing mirror and there he is – the equivalent of Mr Bean on steroids. I say Mr. Bean because these drivers have about as much gumption and general road savvy as our comical friend in his Austin Mini. In fact it doesn't matter if you are in the fast lane doing 120 kilometres per hour, way over the speed limit. Sooner or later, the Thai Evil Kaneval will be there, approximately 6.7 milimetres from your rear bumper, his lights flashing frantically for you to move into another lane and out of his way. As Cent rightly says, Thais have their own style of driving often with scary consequences,

> 'I get to do some serious driving in the LOS [Land of Smiles] during my many times there, and now, as I live there most of the year, I drive all over the place, all over the country. This can be a serious matter if you've ever seen the way some, well most actually, Thais drive. … I saw a pickup truck run a red light right in front of me, broad-siding a woman on her motorcycle, knocking her and her motorcycle

42

clear across the street. Watching her legs slide along the pavement with her motorcycle on top of her, and realizing she's wearing only shorts and a T-shirt, and luckily, a helmet at least, I wince at the thought of the pain she will be in very shortly. I've been there and done that, at 60 mph at that, years ago on my Honda Magna V. Have a bum knee ever since. They were both doing maybe 25 or 30 [kms]. She got clocked good though.' [9]

However if you want to escape this urban madness, you'll find that you are unlikely to fare better using public transport. The infamous tiny green buses that look like a miniature version of a toy from *The Magic Roundabout* are persistent offenders on the roads, too. These are easily the worst drivers to ever hold a bus drivers' license. OK…er…not many of them do actually possess driving licenses I am reliably informed, but no matter. They have been warned so many times to show politeness to other road-users in Thailand, but to no avail. Whether it is an urban myth or not, I don't know, but I have heard it said many times that bus drivers, especially in Bangkok, are usually so stoned out of their heads on meta-amphetamines, what the Thais call *yah-bah*, that they are often oblivious to, not only their passengers, but other road users. The logic goes that they would be unable to drive through that searing heat without something to take their minds off it, and also to keep them awake. Remember this next time you find yourself on one of these buses!

The psychology and general atmosphere whilst using public transport in Thailand is also interesting to think about. When you happen to find yourself on, for example a regular Thai bus, some general considerations need to be noted. The same driver will invariably drive as if he has a prior appointment (which he's only just remembered about), with some mysterious benefactor who is going to alter his and his family's life radically. It is apparently for this reason that he will proceed to slam hard on the brakes at every juncture. It amazes me how these drivers wait till the last second to do this, instead of gently easing on the brakes when approaching a junction. What results is a collective surge of passengers moving forward *en masse* like an unintentional human, as opposed to Mexican Wave. Granny on her weekly visit to feed the ducks in the park gets a new seat on the floor; Somchai, the 7-11 employee gently and apologetically extricates himself from the cleavage of Navaporn, the cute

43

SCB teller; students from nearby colleges hang on for dear life, hoping their hair isn't messed up and make-up isn't smudged when they collide with the stainless steel handrails. The unflappable ticket-collector, almost always a woman, moves slowly down the bus, click-clacks open and shut her klaxon-like metal pencil case full of five and one baht coins, and carries on collecting the money as if nothing ever happened. 'Mai pen rai!' the elderly gentleman mumbles in the corner. 'Amen brother' I say quietly to myself as I pick my self up off the floor!

Bangkok Post journalist, Atiya Achakulwisut, describes it well in her column:

> "Let's face it. Bangkok's public buses have never been a preferred mode of transportation for the city's dwellers. Some are crowded. Others run at unpredictable intervals - two of them may arrive at the same time at the same stop, or you wait an hour and none show up. Some offer a scary ride that can turn your trip into a suicide mission. Others make you feel like being part of a gangster movie - you don't know when the driver or fare collector would take out some hidden weapon (usually it's the long removable gear stick) and storm out of the vehicle to fight some roadside enemy." [10]

What I am trying to suggest, albeit in an exaggerated way is that, though Thai culture is especially polite in situations like this compared to other cultures, there is scant regard for passengers in general on Thai buses or public transport in general. It's very sad, but true. It almost seems as if the driver has the right to drive in whatever way he sees fit, and with total impunity from being reprimanded by the police, his superiors, or even worse still, the passengers themselves. It is in this sense that Embree's notion of loosely woven' as opposed to a 'tightly woven' culture, should be understood, for without this freedom to deviate from what would be considered the norm (e.g. a bus driver taking care of the comfort of his passengers) little would get done in Thai society, and the proverbial wheels of industry would grind to a resounding and decisive halt. Indeed, what you will invariably see after such episodes is the passengers picking themselves up off the floor with the ubiquitous Thai smiles everywhere, and the ever-present exclamations of 'mai bpen rai'. Not a hint of apology

44

ever emanates from the driver, merely a glance in the mirror to survey the scene and check for any damage to the bus.

Getting onto these buses also presents problems of their own. Whilst, as we said, Thai people are among the politest you will ever meet, in certain situations, politeness gives way to something else. Again, before the arrival of the Skytrain, I used to have to travel, on a daily basis, from my home in Pinklao to my office in Siam Square. Getting on the bus outside *Pata*, the department store, was an interesting experience. When the bus arrived, there would be no queue to simply join, but rather a collective rush to get as close to one of the electronic bus doors as possible. In the ensuing melee, jostling and shoving are not uncommon, and actually getting onto the bus quite often involves the use of an elbow or two. Personally, I found middle-aged Thai women to be the most aggressive as they would be almost oblivious to those around them, and indeed push and shove with surprising and alarming skill. If Paradon Srirachapan can play tennis for Thailand, then these women could represent Thailand at bus-hopping! But then you have to remember that the traffic situation in Bangkok adds a lot of time on to daily commuting times for the average citizen, so there is a greater impetus to get on the bus quickly and not have to wait for the next one which of course means you'll have to do it all over again a few minutes later.

You will also see this mini-drama play itself out on the platforms of the BTS. What's interesting about this version is the way people crowd the doors as they arrive at the designated yellow lines. Even with copious signs everywhere, warning them to stand clear of the doors, passengers try to get as close to the door as possible in the hope that they will get on quickly and obtain a seat. It seems to matter not a jot that there are hordes of passengers who have to get off *first* for this to happen. (This happens outside most elevators in Thailand, too.) Such scenes resemble a rugby scrum with one side surging forward to embark, and the other to disembark from the train.

I don't use the Skytrain much these days, but I do remember a time when I was in one of these situations myself. I was getting off at Siam Square and faced the usual hordes of passengers waiting to get on. One woman in particular was hell-bent on getting on, but the only way for her to achieve her aim was for her to literally go *through* me. As there was nowhere for me to go (being surrounded by other passengers, I remembered Tennyson's *Charge of the Light Brigade* poem, "canons to the left, canons to the right…) I continued pushing forward in order to get off the train. Instead of stepping to one side, which would have been the sensible thing to do, this lady tried to push me out of the way. I am sure that, if you haven't seen the movie version of David and Goliath, you are probably familiar with the basic story. Try imagining a short, 40-kilogram, slightly built Asian woman barging into a large, 95-kilogram male and imagine the result. I'm ashamed to say the lady hit the floor like a proverbial 'sack of potatoes'. Embarrassed, I leant down to try to help her to her feet, but she got up by herself and gave me a look that I am unlikely to ever forget. It was something I interpreted as, 'crazy foreigner, you should learn how we do things here'. Fortunately, she wasn't hurt, but one wonders if she learnt something valuable that day? I hope so. I know I did.

Chapter Notes:

[1] Roeland, Philip, *A bit of culture (1)*,
http://www.ajarn.com/Contris/philiproelandjuly2005.htm

[2] Bob, Bangkok, *Bangkok Transport, Getting Around Bangkok*
http://www.bangkokbob.net/transport.htm

[3] Ibid

[4] Ibid

[5] Eliot, T. S., *The Wasteland*,
http://members.cox.net/academia/labelle2.html#eliot

[6] Op Cit, Roeland

[7] Stephen Cleary, *Do's & Don'ts....To Truly Unseen Thailand*, http://www.thai-blogs.com/

[8] Ibid

[9] Cent, *Chok Dee For You And Me*, Stickman's guide to Bangkok Readers' Submissions www.stickmanbangkok.com/Reader/reader1150.html

[10] Atiya Achakulwisut, *A busload of questions on rental scheme*, The *Bangkok Post*, 2009

(Some work being done at a tattoo shop.)

Chapter Four

Superstition and Magic for Thais

Lucky Numbers

So far then, we've looked at many aspects of the Thai way of living and doing. We looked for example, at the Thai predilection for smiling and what that says about them as a polite race of people. We then looked at the dominant group mentality in Thailand, and saw what the different groups mean to their members. It offered us a window into the Thai mindset, and how the Thai collectivist approach to all things impacts greatly on their decision-making processes. From here we saw the hierarchical nature of, and power within, Thai society, a top-down approach, and how it shapes them as a race of people We saw this in the social interactions of members both within and without their culture through the notion of 'personal responsibility'.

As I said in my introduction, it is my view that a culture cannot be understood as a unitary, fixed entity. Indeed, the only way to *truly* understand a race of people is through an understanding of their customs and beliefs, as well as understanding of them as people in an increasingly changing world. And nowhere is there a better key to an understanding of Thai people than in their superstitions, for they are in many respects like the Ireland of yesteryear with a strong belief in fairies and magic. Whether we are talking about marriage, death, gambling, sport, or shopping, Thais, as we shall see, have a superstition for every occasion.

Numbers:

Unquestionably, Thai (especially Thai-Chinese) people are the most superstitious people I have ever met. Numbers, because of the large

Chinese influence in Thailand, have their own mythology. As Piset Wattanavitukul explains,

> 'Among the Caozhou overseas Chinese in Thailand, it is customary to give a cash sum that ends with the number 4 to married couples. "44" is pronounced *"shi shi"* meaning "every generation or eternity." "104" therefore means "100 life times". This carries a blessing for the married couple to be in love for 100 life times or forever. Interestingly however, my friends in China were shocked to hear that I planned to use this number for a friend who was getting married. In China *"shi"* would be interpreted as meaning "death".'[1]

Moreover, when, for example, you wear amulets, you should also wear odd numbers each time because even numbers (like 2, 4, 6 amulets and so on) are used by Buddhist monks at funerals. Therefore, it's often not considered good luck to wear even-numbered amulets.

Evil Spirits:

Superstitious practices predate even the Chinese influence, even before the major influx into Thailand of Chinese immigrants in the 1920s and 1930s. Local Thais, especially from the North-east of Thailand, have a long history of superstitious practices, too. If you imagine the traditional teak houses built on stilt-like beams, you would perhaps have assumed it was primarily to keep high above any risk of flooding, a regular problem in the North-east of Thailand; but there was another reason, too,

> 'According to superstition and traditional Thai belief, the raised thresholds of Thai houses prevent evil spirits from creeping in at night and disrupting the sleep of the inhabitants. It also served a functional purpose.' [2]

General superstitions:

Here are just a few of the more general though no less unusual superstitions well known among Thai people courtesy of Richard Barrow,

(1) Do not take off a ring from someone else's finger because you will be taking away the people they love.

(2) Do not spit in the toilet because you will have a mole on your lips.

(3) Do not spit towards the sky because it is a sin.

(4) Do not pluck your eyebrows during the evening because bad things will happen to you.

(5) Do not plough on holy days because the rice won't grow.

(6) Do not say to a baby that they are cute because the ghost will come and take the baby away.

(7) Do not break anything on your wedding day because it is a sign that your marriage won't last.

(8) Do not drop chopsticks during the Chinese New Year because you won't make a good living.

(9) Do not let a woman sit on a staircase for a long time because she will have a difficult labour.

(10) Do not sit higher than a monk because it is a sin.

(11) Do not sit on the big water jars because it is a sin.

(12) Do not sit on pillows meant for your head because you will get a painful rash on your behind.

(13) Do not count off the names of people that have died because you will be next.

(14) Do not keep anything belonging to the temple inside your house because a disaster will happen to you.

(15) Do not offer the same food to your dead ancestors and to the monks because you will then rot in hell. [3]

Some of them are intriguing for the obvious value of the advice given therein. Take number (9) as an example, 'Do not let a woman sit on a staircase for a long time because she will have a difficult labour.' This one is fairly obvious in the sense that if you sit on cold, hard areas, you'll inevitably end up with varicous veins and are probably likely to develop hemorrhoids as well; neither of which are exactly conducive to a trouble-free pregnancy. Number (6) is merely a version of the Third Eye myth prevalent in many countries [4] And my favourite which is number (8) 'Do not drop chopsticks during the Chinese New Year because you won't make a good living.'

Travel:

Another area of superstitions involves travel and the small geckos that are omnipresent in Thailand called the *jink jock*. This piece of advice is amusing:

> '...if you are going out on an important trip to do some important business, you should step out of the house using your right foot. If you hear a gecko singing when you are going out, then it is a very bad sign and you should not go out...'[5]

(On the subject of lizards, for example, if you hear a *Took Gare* (a type of gecko) call out nine times in one go, then you can make a wish. (Whether it comes true or not is another matter!)

Getting a lucky number for your car is also highly prized as it can apparently prolong your life and protect you from accidents much like the Saint Christopher medals that westerners place in their car dashboards. Actually, a priest will be sought to put a traditional offering of some kind, often a jasmine garland, on the rear view mirror, along with some coloured pieces of cloth and painted lucky symbols on the steering wheel and ceiling of the car.

> 'In August 2003, Thailand's Land Transport Department organised the country's first ever auction of uncommon and lucky license plates to address complaints that corrupt officials were secretly selling lucky numbers or giving them to well-connected patrons. Communications minister Suriya Jungrungraungkit attended the auction, and left with the coveted number 9999. His high bid? Four million baht (£59,000 for lucky license plate).' [6]

Asking a monk to come to your house to bless a new car is very common. It is probably a good idea however to consult the monk before you buy your car in order to find out the exact day and hour it is deemed auspicious to bring your car to your house for the first time. People who are often dismissive about the powers of a blessing to protect the car and its occupants often rush out to get a blessing after the car has been involved in an accident. Although, as others have said, 'this is like locking the stables doors after the horse has bolted.' [7]

Visiting Fortune Tellers:

As a teacher, I have many times felt obliged to mildly admonish students for being late to class. Although it would have been rare to have actually heard it right there and then from the tardy students themselves (because Thais, as we saw in Chapter Two, will revert to 'white lies' in order to preserve a degree of calm and order), the reason is that they had been to visit a *maw doo* or fortune teller. Like the monks, fortune tellers play a major part of Thai life in matters of general, day-to-day advice giving, or in matters spiritual, and this is on the increase in times of uncertainty. As Srisamporn Poosuphanusorn says, 'When Thai people face uncertainty, many go to fortune tellers for predictions.'

Unsurprisingly, with the political turmoil in which Thailand has been imboiled over the last few years, the numbers of Thais visiting a *maw doo* or using their services in some other way has increased dramatically. One new way is via mobile phones. Isoon Thiraniti from the Shineedotcom horoscope centre says, 'Up to 2,000 customers call our service number per day, 30% of which were repeat clients, thanks to our professional team of fortune tellers.' [8]

Indeed, there is a huge market that now services this part of the Thai consumer market, as Mr. Issoon says,

> '... the fortune-telling market was expected to double to two billion baht this year, thanks to the economic slump, political pressure and social problems. Shinee expects to see 100 million baht from fortune-telling services out of total revenue of 200 million this year.' [9]

Amulets or lucky charms:

There are many other examples of the way Thais live by mystical or magical codes like, as I said in my introduction, the Irish have done throughout the centuries. The first is connected to the Buddhist amulets, which are worn by many Thais in the kingdom. These are said to ward off evil spirits and protect the owner from any impending disaster. Here's what Michael Buckley has to say on the subject,

> 'Apart from appeasing the traffic gods, there are myriad other forms of warding off trouble in Bangkok, from supplicating at key Buddha statues to wearing tiny Buddha amulets around the neck. These amulets can be multipurpose or can be specifically blessed by an abbot for protection against bullets, knives, ghosts, or wild animals.' [10]

Go to almost any market from Chinatown to Pratunam and you will see these miniature amulets on sale. So valuable to Thai people are they that there are some who would accept no price for their sale. As Michael Buckley explains,

> 'Miraculous stories about the supernatural powers of amulets grace the pages of half a dozen magazines in Bangkok devoted solely to these charms. One that was translated for me showed a taxi driver shot by a high-powered gun at close range, but the bullet didn't even pierce his skin, just left him with a burn mark and a bruise. The driver claims his amulet saved his life.' [11]

This particular belief in the power of amulets is often found in Thai movies, too. Take for example the well-known Thai movie *Fun Bar Karaoke*, [12] which deals with Pu, a young Thai lady who works for an advertising agency. She lives with her father: a playboy who likes to frequent karaoke bars Recently, she has been having a strange dream, *fan ba*, about her dead mother, who, in the dream, has continued building a house for them all to live in.

Despite living in a complex postmodern environment and working in a highly vibrant business sector, Pu is a traditional Thai girl, a family-oriented dutiful daughter, and full of old-fashioned superstitions. The dream keeps coming back to haunt her whether she is awake or asleep, and she simply cannot steer her mind away from it. With assistance from Pum, her only friend, whose mother is a fortune-teller and works as a 7-11 store clerk, Pu decides to seek advice concerning her mysterious dream from Pum's father. The fortune-teller tells Pu that if the dream continues, her father will soon die when the house is finished. His advice makes Pu sick with worry about her father's fate. Here's what Pattana Kitiars says,

> 'Although Pu's father possesses expensive and most auspicious Buddha amulets as advertised by the amulet dealer, supernatural power fails to save him from the life-threatening misfortunes by [his enemies] the chao pho's cronies. The law of karma shows its obvious force against Pu's Father. He suffers the consequences of his own fun-loving behaviour as well as his neglect of his paternal responsibility at home.' [13]

Spirit Houses:

Another aspect of Thai superstition is to seen in the spirit houses that are both inside and outside of most Thai houses, hotels, bars, and indeed any buildings that are occupied by Thais. The Thai name for the one outside the building is *Saan Jao* and is for the spirit of the land. However, you also have *Hing Phra* inside, which is used to pay respect to Buddha. Offerings such as food (mostly fruit) are placed inside these structures as a sign of respect.

Death:

Another aspect is the Thai notion or acceptance of Death. As with all deaths when they are in the public domain, people usually flock to the scene to gawk or to get a glimpse of the tragic act, and in this respect, Thais are no different from anyone else. However, Thais seem to be affected in quite different ways to such a grim occurrence. I have witnessed a few road accidents in my time here and am amazed at the way

Thais view death, so much so that I am convinced that they have a completely different regard for this phenomenon ontologically speaking. Indeed, one of the most common sights when watching the behaviour of Thai people around say, a traffic accident, is to see them asking about e.g. the age of the victim, the digits on the number plate of the vehicle, the age of the driver etc. I'll let an anonymous reader of *The Bangkok Post* explain why they do this and the difference in behaviour between westerners and Thais when it comes to Death,

> 'The difference I'm talking about is in regard to a tragic occurrence in a condo here in Thailand. A large crowd of farang expats, Thai students and middle to upper class Thais had gathered to find out why an ambulance and many policemen were gathered on the soi in front of a high-rise condominium. Tragically, a young Thai female had jumped to her death from a high floor in this condominium. Westerners were talking about how tragic it was for such a young girl to be now lying dead on the street. They were speculating whether it was an accident or suicide. Some foreigners were emotionally moved and expressed deep sorrow for the girl's parents and family. Many were asking what would make a young person do such a thing and what could be done to prevent it from happening again? What I saw with the farang was a deep concern for the dead young girl, for her parents and family, and for other young people facing situations that they couldn't overcome. On the other hand, the conversations between the Thais were about ghosts and superstitions: whether living or being near this condo was bad luck and they were talking about being afraid to live in the condo or even visit friends they knew who lived in that particular condo. But, amazingly, their conversations didn't stop at ghosts and superstitions. To my total amazement and disgust, many of the Thai people were actively trying to find out the age of the young girl and the floor from which she jumped. For the life of me, I couldn't understand why the age of the girl and the floor she jumped from were so important – until I overheard a well-dressed, middle-aged Thai lady say that she wanted the age of the girl and the floor she jumped from so she could go and buy lottery tickets with those combinations of numbers.' [14]

Of course this story does not reflect the way all Thai people behave around death, but it does show, albeit anecdotally, a reaction that is not entirely uncommon.

Sport:

In sport too, we see a semblance of the Thai uneasiness in allowing females to take part in what is a quite dangerous and brutally violent sport as Jennifer Gampell explains,

> 'Superstition and prejudice color the Thai attitude
> toward female boxers. Let women anywhere near
> a boxing ring and supposedly they'll jinx it.' [15]

One personal experience of Thai superstition happened when I had not been long in the kingdom and had been given the unenvious privilege of teaching the deputy head of the Thai Ministry of Education and his wife. They were both very nice, polite, and courteous at all times and very eager to learn. They had been given free lessons by the owner of the school in order for the teaching licences of the teachers to go smoothly through the education department. One day however, they both came into the room, sat down and the lesson began. A couple of times, I noticed the lady put her nose in the air as if trying to catch a whiff of something, but I just assumed she had caught the smell of some Thai dish owing to the fact that the classroom was right next to the canteen where people could be seen eating from the windows of the classroom. I was wrong. A few minutes later, the lady leaned over to her husband and whispered in his ear. They then looked at me and asked, 'can you smell anything?' I replied that 'no' I couldn't. A further few minutes went by, and then I heard a shriek as the lady jumped up from the desk and pulled her husband with her. Underneath the desk was a huge rat, the size of an over-fed cat and it had obviously been dead for some time as the stench had by now become quite obvious. They were really unnerved by this thinking it some omen and alas I never saw them again.

Of course, whilst it is easy to dismiss these superstitions as mere fable, they do underlie an aspect that is uniquely Thai. Chulalongkorn University historian, Sunait Chutintaranond, explains that superstitions come easily to the Thai people at this time and function as an antidote to materialism. 'People are seeking something to rely on when they are losing their jobs or don't have money for their children's schooling.'[16]

Likewise, Kriengsak Charoenwongsak, an academic, author, Christian and director of the Institute of Future Studies for Development says,

> 'Thirty years of development, with consumerism at its core, have driven the Thai people to a place where they are dry spiritually…The rat race has caused people to think what is the point of all these material things? They are missing something. But they don't know what they are looking for.' [17]

Whatever the need for superstitions in Thai life, one thing is for sure they are as quintessential to Thais as Jasmine rice or Tom Yam Goong.

Chapter Notes:

[1] Wattanavitukul, Piset, *Rainbow Chasing Dragons Lucky Chinese Numbers and Words and How to Use Them,* February 2002, http://www.apmforum.com/columns/china17.htm

[2] *Fascinating aspects of the Thai House, Keeping Evil Spirits Out and Babies* http://www.jimthompsonhouse.com/museum/fascinat.asp

[3] *Barrow, Richard,* Richard's Life in Thailand, Thai Superstitions http://www.thai-blogs.com/index.php/2005/09/20/thai_superstitions?blog=5

[4] See this website for an account of The Third Eye Myth, http://www.moebius.nl/content/blogcategory/103/263/

[5] Thailand QA forum
http://www.thailandqa.com/forum/archive/index.php/t-1429.html

[6] £59,000 for lucky license plate
http://www.cronaca.com/archives/week_2003_08_10.html

[7] Blessing a Car, http://www.thailandlife.com/car.html

[8] *Fortune tellers set to profit from uncertainty*, Bangkok Post, Monday October 15, 2007 http://www.bangkokpost.com/

[9] Ibid

[10] Buckley, Michael, *Thailand's Talismans Cast a Wide Net of Protection*, 21-Apr-2005 http://www.straight.com/content.cfm?id=9625

[11] Ibid

[12] Ratanaruang, Pen-Ek, Director, Fun Bar Karaoke (literally "dream crazy karaoke") 1997 http://en.wikipedia.org/wiki/Fun_Bar_Karaoke

[13] Kitiars, Pattana, *Faiths and Films: Crisis of Thai Buddhism on the Silver Screen*

http://216.239.51.104/search?q=cache:niRMoqA8xEIJ:scbs.stanford.edu/c alendar/200304/burma_conference/papers/kitiarsa.doc+Thais+and+Supers tition+&hl=en

[14] Anonymous reader, *The Bangkok Post*,

http://www.bangkokpost.com/

[15] Gampell, Jennifer, *Thailand's Boxing Babes, Women Make Their Way Back into the Ring* in Weekend Journal: *The Asian Wall Street Journal*, July 14-16, 2000 http://gampell.com/boxing.htm

[16] Quoted in, Gearing, Julian, *A Royal to the Rescue*, http://www.asiaweek.com/asiaweek/99/0416/feat4.html

[17] Ibid

(Some KPMG employees hard at work in their office in Bangkok.)

Chapter Five

Thais in the Office

The Office Jay

'**E**k-cue me? You want tape, copy two?' I look back at Jay, the Thai office technician, quizzically. 'Yes', I say. 'Two copies.' He scratches his head.
'Solly, no have. Mai mee!'
'Ok, one copy then?' He scratches his head again.
'But I requested them two weeks ago, in writing'. He scratches his head a third time, smiles profusely, and timidly walks away.

This scene must have played itself out in thousands of companies up and down the length and breadth of Thailand, and illustrates something that is as quintessential to the Thais as jasmine rice - the DIY principle: if you want something done, and it's important, wherever and whenever possible, do it yourself. It's simply no good waiting and expecting someone to do it for you, even if that is in fact part of their job remit. But be careful, though: doing someone else's job could mean that that person loses face, and such a situation presents a Pandora's Box of unmentionables for you to have to deal with later if it becomes known by other Thai employees. Do it by all means, but do it with stealth, lest you trod on someone's toes and create bad feeling in your office.

Now, ordinarily, this particular oversight by Jay would not have been a problem for me. I have been in this kind of situation many times in my many years in the kingdom. However, seeing as this is the morning of a midterm listening test, whereby, when I enter the classroom, I will see about thirty expectant faces hanging on my every word and instruction, it means that things have in fact become a major problem. I rush around like an overworked Man-Friday on meta-amphetamines, picking up this paper, photocopying this master sheet, searching drawers for additional copies of the tape. Eventually, the situation is under control, and I walk into my classroom a paragon of refined elegance and undisturbed languor.

As I said, these and other such happenings are everyday occurrences for the average western employee in Thailand, and there are many reasons why. The first and perhaps main reason is that salaries in Thailand are quite low relative to many other Asian countries, which means that getting skilled local workers is not always easy given budget constraints. Another reason is that training, whether it be on the job training, or pre-job training is not something that has great emphasis placed upon it here. Indeed, employers prefer to hire local staff members, which are likely to 'fit in', or who already have a connection with somebody in the company. Thus our employee above, Jay, is a member of a prolific group of employees who, for many farangs, simply don't 'cut the mustard' but who, nevertheless, are tolerated even respected in the company and among their Thai colleagues for a variety of reasons. The most prolific of these is because he or she is a member of a well-known family and thus has strong connections, as Sununta Siengthai makes clear,

> 'With respect to staffing, while family members generally
> fill almost all of the upper-tier positions in these organizations,
> middle and even lower-tier positions are typically filled by
> those who have connections with family members.' [1]

Actually, this practice is endemic in Thailand and goes part of the way in explaining why I've had to bring my car back to the garage two weeks after it has *apparently* been serviced (Somchai the mechanic never actually studied mechanics – he just happened to know the garage owner's cousin and was unemployed when the regular mechanic departed for greener pastures). Equally, when I go to a Mall and ask for information (in Thai) about one of the products, I get the head-scratching scene all over again. Incidentally, this lack of any discernible training is from the same sales assistant who has just been following me around the aisles for the last 5 minutes, much to my chagrin.

Although I do not entirely agree with the following, it does have a certain ring of truth to it as I have had personal experience of this a number of times myself. Caveman explains,

> 'How many times have you read about the fact that most Thai business owners would rather employ 10 incompetent workers at cheap wage rates than 1 competent worker at a higher rate? Well, this factor will have the effect of making it "OK" to be incompetent, and will do nothing to provide an incentive for workers to excel and put forth maximum effort in the workplace. This impacts important things like worker productivity, customer satisfaction, and maybe even job tenure. This is one of the big reasons that wages are so low in Thailand: because it is not expected that most workers will really contribute anything significant to the business. If they even try, chances are that they will not last long anyway, because they might be viewed as too "cavalier", exposing upper management for its lameness and making them lose face. Worker mediocrity is the norm.'[2]

Caveman has a point here, but he fails to understand the way Thais see themselves in the office. For Thais, as we've seen, (Chapter Two) human relationships are far more important than whether a company is efficient or not, or whether someone forgot to do a task that was formally requested. These tasks are perceived by Thais as merely minor details, office gloss, temporary aberrations that go nowhere to promoting a good feeling in the office. On the contrary, for the average Thai, a certain lightness of being should be prevalent, a certain light, airy, fun atmosphere should be the norm in the office, or as Suntaree Komin says, an 'outward presentation of the "fun" and the "lightness" approach to things of the Thai.' [3]

For Suntaree, this Thai aspect of fun-loving, take-it-easy approach to work varies among the populace and also whether one is a government employee or not,

'It is the Bangkokians and particularly the government officials who preferred fun-loving over work, and are generally known to be very lax and inefficient in job performance. As for the fun-leisure and "smiling" aspect, it can be explained as the resulting behavioral pattern from keeping a pleasant and smooth face-to-face interpersonal interaction, which is a higher value. In so doing, most Thai social interactions are pleasant, light, might be superficial, yet fun and humorous in nature.' [4]

Moreover, Thais don't need an incentive to excel and put forth maximum effort in the workplace as Caveman put it. This is because they are usually more concerned with making sure their boss and co-workers are happy, or that some aspect of the office rumour-mill is *not* currently focusing on them. Putting in long hours, being prepared to cancel a prior appointment in order to work late, or working weekends at short notice, are just some of the things that Thais know are expected of them. In other words, in an office situation, quantity is often a more important factor than quality – being available to work long hours is more important than what tangible element of worker productivity is produced, per se, so the notions of competency/incompetency that Caveman mentions above are redundant given the Thai position of what constitutes good office practice.

Indeed, whilst westerners are brought up to seek out experiences that lead to a sense of accomplishment, a degree of personal achievement, the very notion of words like 'achievement' have a completely different connotation when translated into Thai. What this means is that the average Thai has little or no sense of what that is, neither in a personal, nor in an office context, certainly not in the way a westerner would have. As Suntaree Komin rightly explains,

'One striking fact about the concept of "achievement" is that the work itself is not translatable in many non-English speaking cultures as in Thai language; particularly the Thai word for ambition (*tayurr tayaan*) has a negative connotation for Thai personality.' [5]

Another misconception that is often mentioned about Thais in the office is the fact that Thais never accept responsibility for anything. Whilst this is partially true, there are a number of factors that should be taken into consideration. The first is that collectivist societies in general do not place a great emphasis on individuals taking responsibility because, by and large, everything is done with the group in mind, and if a mistake is made, it is in some sense perceived as a mistake of the group. Moreover, as those at the upper send of the hierarchy are not only more respected, but paid more too, it follows that they should be the ones to take responsibility when things go awry. As Theerasak Thanasankit says,

> 'Thai subordinates usually do not feel comfortable with making decisions. As we mentioned earlier, decision-making is their superiors' duty. Therefore, making a decision about approving further requirements gathering or approving the requirements themselves was passed to upper managerial levels to make the decision. This situation can exist even though the committee agrees with the requirements identified. However, the members of the reference committee do not feel comfortable with approving the requirements because being involved in the decision making process may bring them unwanted responsibility'. [6]

This is illustrated by a short dialogue below:

Interviewee: … when I worked with one company that was medium sized…there was only one boss, and the rest were workers in technical, software and hardware areas. The boss wanted the workers to take responsibility in developing the system. It was not right. I had to be the boss who takes responsibility in developing the system and understand the whole system and confirm it with everyone. So no one wanted to sign any documents.
Interviewer: They are afraid that if the system does not work then it will be their fault?
Interviewee: Yes. [7]

Here then we have the crux of the problem. The clearly defined hierarchical nature of Thailand necessitates that only those at the top are required to be *fully* responsible for any mishaps in the workplace. The average Thai, on the other hand, feels he or she need only do their best for the company, and if they should happen to get into a problem area, then the management or superiors should not only sort out the problem, but also shoulder the bulk of the responsibility. Theerasak continues to explain this idea,

'The social construction of authority and acceptance of responsibility in elicitation in organisations in Thailand reflects the hierarchical nature of society and more especially the construction of responsibility at the top. Since responsibility was always upwards, requirements approval was always delayed and sometimes inhibited.' [8]

In a survey conducted by a leading business forum group in Thailand, when asked what bothered them most about Thai employees, western managers answered in the following way. They ranked the following statement 15th out of 32 as a 'weakness of Thais' with whom they have worked, which they 'would like them to change'

'Not taking responsibility for workloads at critical times.' [9]

Other, complaints ranged from 'Reactive work methods rather than proactive (requires more supervision)' (17th), 'Not alerting their *farang* boss about a problem until the disaster has or is about to strike' (21st), and 'Failure to separate personal and professional life' (3rd). [10]

There is also a marked difference in the values that each employee sets on his or her place in the overall structure within the company. Whereas westerners place skill, personal responsibility, and foresight ahead of almost anything related to their jobs, Thais value commitment and their time. Moreover, Thais value loyalty over competence, but they also want the security of the acknowledgement of senior rank, too. It is here that the implicit hierarchy that underpins Thai society comes into focus. Henry Holmes and Suchada Tangtongtavy explain this well,

'A second related issue is the stress often placed by multinationals on competence as compared with loyalty as a criterion for promotion or even retention. Thais generally recognize the need for competence, but feel that seniority should be valued, too. Many believe that a person who has been around for years can be trusted

69

to protect his boss, the company, and precious company information'.[11]

Clearly, then there are marked differences in perception as to what the role of employees is in the East and the West. In the latter, we are used to seeing the employee as a cog in a wheel, as an integral, yet independent element in making sure that the company is successful in producing both qualitatively and quantatively whatever its product is. In the former, the emphasis is primarily on simply being there and being available at all times, and of course showing loyalty. How then does the western manager fare when trying to get the Thai employees to adopt the western mindset? The same western manager was asked the following,

Question:'What have you done that successfully changed Thai staff to improve their performance?'

Answer: 'I try to make it clear where the responsibility for completing a task lies, particularly one which is repeated each month. My main aim is to make each team-member as self-sufficient as possible with regard to their day-to-day tasks. I try to stress that it is not my job to tell them what to do in every case. [12]

And again, the answer to the same question,

Question:'What have you done that successfully changed Thai staff to improve their performance?'

Answer: 'Sacked incompetent staff who hold back the organization.' [13]

What is clear then is that there are many areas in which Thais and westerners differ with regards to work. As we have seen, for the Thais, work is something that occupies a great deal of their time, and which crosses over into their family lives, where the job itself will almost be an extension of their family lives given the amount of time spent there; for the Thai, a job is something you *have*, but for a westerner, it is something you *do*.

On a personal note, I once worked for a company, which was owned by an extremely rich Thai-Chinese lady and her husband. They had businesses all over the world, from Germany to China, and from Indonesia to

Belgium. Making money was for them primarily a game. They would bet each other paltry sums of money to see who could make the most from the companies they controlled in any given quarter of a financial year. This particular company was the responsibility of the Thai-Chinese lady herself. The husband was nowhere to be seen. What I noticed was the way she treated her employees. There was always a relaxed atmosphere, and all the staff seemed to get along quite well.

What was curious though was her management style. On one occasion, a motorcycle courier who had worked for her for several years simply disappeared. Nobody knew where he went. Some thought he'd been arrested and ended up in jail. Calls were made but no answers found to this apparent anomaly. One day, however three weeks later the said motorcycle courier turns up for work and walks casually in the door as if nothing had happened. The Thais, being the polite souls everyone knows they are, simply avoided any difficult questions, and greeted him in exactly the same way. The Thai-Chinese-lady also carried on in much the same vein. Clearly, sacking the employee was not something she seriously considered, although in the West, he'd probably have been, if not grilled by the boss about his extended absence, fired in a heartbeat.

I heard another story one day, this one about one of an office owner and manager and her former accountant. He had been caught stealing from her; with his hand in the proverbial cookie jar. It was discovered that he'd been 'cooking the books' for some time, unobserved by anyone. What did she do upon hearing the news? She reported him to the police. There was a court case whereupon the accountant agreed to pay back the stolen sum of money in return for immunity from a jail sentence. What happened next however completely astounded me. The accountant was re-employed. What this says about Thai employers and loyalty is anyone's guess!

Chapter Notes:

[1] Siengthai, Sununta, *HR Practices in Southeast Asia*
http://www.asdu.ait.ac.th/faculty/FacultyByID.cfm?FacultyID=255

[2] Caveman, *A Caveman's Point Of View Of The Thai Economy*
http://www.stickmanbangkok.com/reader/reader209.html

[3] Komin, Suntaree, *Psychology of the Thai People : Values and Behavioral Patterns* (1990) in *NATIONAL CHARACTER IN THE THAI NINE VALUES ORIENTATIONS.*
http://studyinthailand.org/study_abroad_thailand_university/Suntaree/suntaree_komin_2.html

[4] Op Cit, Siengthai, Sununta

[5] Ibid, Komin, Suntaree

[6] Thanasankit, Theerasak, and Corbitt, Brian, *Cultural Context and its Impact on Requirements Elicitation in Thailand*, EJISDC (2000) 1, 2, 1-19 The Electronic Journal on Information Systems in Developing Countries,
http://www.ejisdc.org/ojs2/index.php/ejisdc/article/view/2

[7] Ibid

[8] Ibid

[9] Niratpattanasai, Kriengsak *Expatriate Perceptions of Thai Colleagues - Survey Results* http://www.apmforum.com/columns/thai45.htm

[10] Ibid – Kriengsak, Survey Results

[11] Holmes, Henry and Tangtongtavy, Suchada, *Working with the Thais,* White Lotus Co., Limited, 1995

[12] Op. Cit, Kriengsak, *Expatriate Perceptions of Thai Colleagues - Survey Results* http://www.apmforum.com/columns/thai45.htm

[13] Ibid, Kriengsak, Survey Results

(Hanchai Hamrin and Ashley Priest teach some Thai students)

Chapter Six

Thais and Education

E=Education²

"It is the supreme art of the teacher to awaken joy in creative expression and knowledge." (Albert Einstein)

When asked about his educational background and academic learning, a young Albert Einstein famously said 'The only thing interfering with my learning, is my education'. [1] By this, Einstein meant that education in some sense stifles true learning or knowledge, and that the best place to learn is *not* always in a school. In fact, Einstein was highly critical of the educational practices of his day, some of which included a lack of creative teaching practices, learning by rote, and extreme punishment for miscreants. What's interesting though is that some of these same practices still exist in Thailand today. Although Einstein went on to become not only a great scholar, but a great teacher too, we shouldn't undervalue his achievement in becoming a genius *despite* his education.

But the point still stands: Thais are amazing people *despite* their education not because of it. How then can we square that with the fact that Thailand has never produced any world renowned geniuses? By world renowned geniuses, I mean people who are not only incredibly smart and made a significant contribution to their own country, but who have also made a significant contribution to some aspect of the world. And here's the rub. How do you rise out of your educational limitations? How do you maximize what your school and your teaching environment provides for you?

They say that if you give a hundred primates an infinite amount of time and a typewriter, then sooner or later, they'll produce the equivalent of Shakespeare. [2] With that idea in mind, one wonders how long it would take for Thailand to produce one Einstein? One Bill Gates? One Steve Jobs? It is hard to fathom why this hasn't already happened. After all, aren't Thais clever enough? Don't they always produce outstanding students especially in the sciences? A resounding 'yes' must be the obvious answer to both questions.

Look at any of the world league tables just for mathematics and you'll see Asians are always at the top of the list, so it is clear that there is no shortage of ability, certainly not in the area of math and science. So, just what is it then that stops Thailand being at the forefront of great science, great art, or great literature?

When you think of England, you think of Newton, Wordsworth, and Morris; when you think of the USA, you think of Franklin, Edison, and Whitman; when you think of Thailand, not that many names roll of the tongue. Just what it is it that stops Thailand from producing its own great scientists, writers, artists, even great athletes for that matter? The answer relates to the culture, education, and the inherent unfairness in the system

There are many reasons why Thai students, not only the brightest ones, find it difficult to excel and get the education they deserve: poor teaching methods, low quality facilities, croneyism, nepotism, Tea Money, but to name the most obvious ones.

Only just recently I read about a case in which a former prime minister and several other politicians were accused of buying their degrees or having a poorly paid academic 'ghost write' their postgraduate theses for them in return for cash. [3] Is it any wonder then that a practice of buying education affords disadvantages to those from poorer backgrounds when they are confronted with this lack of a level playing field?

Similarly, the old chestnut, Tea Money, is yet another reason why Thailand is not producing the bright young talents, the entrepreneurs of the future. For those not familiar with this practice, I'll let another explain. Originally, the practice of giving tea money came from the public sector and probably seemed quite harmless even innocuous at first, as Dennis Coday remarks,

'To access public services, poor people had to pay
"tea money," so called because public servants would
say they needed a little cash for their afternoon tea. It
might take just 30 or 40 baht (less than a dollar) to get
a document notarized at the local government or to take
care of a minor driving violation, but for the working
poor that could mean a quarter to a half a day's wages.'[4]

This practice of 'a little cash for their afternoon tea' then became widespread, especially in the education sector when Little Somchai's entrance into a well established school depended on what in football parlance is called a 'bung', or a 'kickback' if you're a businessman. This was the aim of the new constitution created in 2000. The aim of the new law was the following:

'As Thailand wrestles with the concept of a Constitution designed to erode centuries of corruption, a historic ruling by the Thai State Council on April 26 delivered a small but important lesson. In deeming that quotas allowing privileged students admission to leading schools were discriminatory, the council assured Thais that the new Constitution was not just about cleaning up government and politicians. It was about creating an even playing field for all citizens.' [5]

In my many years in the Kingdom, I have seen how highly valued education is in Thailand. There can be no question that teachers are awarded a very high status. Being a teacher is not just a job; it's a position in society. Further, a teacher is always addressed as 'Ajarn', a label that carries with it a high degree of respect, be it within the confines of the university, at social functions, by neighbours, or by the local shopkeeper.

Yet, for all the respect and esteem afforded to teacher, foreign or local, I have seen how young Thais are not only *not* encouraged to be independent, to stand out or be different, the way they would be in the west, but they are actively *discouraged* to be so. They are taught only Asian values: to fit in, to respect their elders, and most importantly, not to excel by spending time alone doing other things that might be self fulfilling but *not* beneficial to the group. Is it any wonder then that they do not excel at activities, which require self-discipline, focus, motivation and genuine single-mindedness? As I said before, the Thai word for ambition (*tayurr tayaan*) has itself a negative connotation in Thai.

The cultural side of the problem relates to what I said in Chapter Two about the Thais having a heightened sense of their own self, what Komin calls, '…a very big ego, a deep sense of independence, pride and dignity. They cannot tolerate any violation of the "ego" self.' It naturally follows that losing face is very much to be avoided.

It is an old adage, but like so many adages, there is a degree of truth in them as the following will demonstrate – 'you can't make an omellete without first breaking an egg.' In other words, something often needs to break first before it can be fixed. In my opinion, something needs to *give* in the Thai education sector, a major overhaul needs to take place, a few eggs need to be cracked (and a few rotten ones removed) if Thailand is to ever produce its own share of people in the world, the movers and shakers, who change the world we live in. But before that happens, a radical change in mindset, along with a more modern educational system needs to be installed within the country. As Nick Tarver says,

> 'I believe that the problems mentioned […] stem
> ultimately from the fear of 'losing face'. It is this
> fear that holds the education system back. What can
> be done about this? Unfortunately, little can be done
> to change an adult's already indoctrinated mind, but
> there certainly is hope for the students. They need to
> be encouraged to ask questions and not fear failure in
> front of other people. Ultimately they need to be told
> that short-term failure can actually be a catalyst for
> long-term success, and losing face now might actually
> preserve face in the future.' [6]

But just how ingrained is this concept within the Thai psyche? I have seen innumerable times the way Thai students lower their heads to avoid a confrontation or act very submissively when they perceive that the spotlight is on them. There really is no way to enable them to confront a problem head on when they have been ingrained since birth to do the opposite. As Margaret Ukosakul states,

'It is interesting to note that a large number of Thai 'face' idioms describe shame or anger. Shame is therefore closely interconnected to the Thai concept of face. Shame is also used in the Thai society as a social sanction to make people conform to the acceptable norms of society.' [7]

One thing is for sure though. Nowadays, with the widespread influence of globalisation, all that old style charm that the Thais have been famous for is changing, and not just in the Higher Education sector. You only have to look at the growth in the Private Sector of what are usually termed 'progressive' teaching methodologies from bastions of education like the Montessori, Emilio Reggio, and Waldorf schools. These approaches to education put the child at the center of learning process and place great emphasis on the teacher developing the natural instincts and inclinations of the child in their own learning practices. At current estimates, there are at least twelve of these schools at kindergarden or pre-school level in Bangkok alone, at least twenty-six international schools in Bangkok to add to that list, along with a further sixty-four international schools across Thailand. [8]

Although, I have been mostly happy with the level of facilities and support in my time teaching in Thailand, this has not always been so. I remember when I had returned from a short stint in Japan and was looking for some teaching work. I recall going for an interview at a school near Pinklao. It was also a teachers' training college as I remember. I was with my English girlfriend at the time, who had proffered certificates from a college in Oxford. Not *the* Oxford you understand, as in Oxford University, but another one in the same city. The principal of the college, the interviewer, a Dean no less, picked up her degree certificate and looked at it like it was a map to secret treasure, the way Japanese people look at newly acquired business cards at a first meeting. We knew we had the job right there and then. For him, the word 'Oxford' was like having the key to a new world. We got a tour of the college and a tour of the library. The only problem here was that there weren't all that many books. I remember picking up a copy of Byron's poetry and a book about how to mend a punctured tyre. The rest of the books, and there weren't that many, were all in Thai.

Two weeks later we got our class lists: the average was between 50-65 students. We had been told about 30-35. We were shell-shocked and couldn't imagine how we were going to teach in a school where books didn't seem to matter; no students had books either so no syllabus, and we would have to use a microphone to reach the students at the back of the room. In despair, we resigned before we had even started, I think mostly, because we were simply overwhelmed with the task that lay in front of us.

When you look at the overall quality of teaching in Thai schools too, some surprising facts emerge. As the Thailand correspondent for the *English Language Gazette*, in 2010, I reported on some tests carried out by the Office of the Basic Education Council (OBEC) to see whether the teachers themselves knew their subjects well enough to teach them. The results were nothing short of shocking.

"This year saw testing among teachers at the senior high school level, but red flags began appearing immediately. With a pass mark of 59 per cent, the vast majority of teachers failed their subjects miserably. According to figures released by the Office of the Basic Education Commission (OBEC), as many as 88 per cent of the 3,973 teachers surveyed whose speciality is computer sciences failed the test. A similar fail rate was found among teachers of biology, maths and physics tested in their specialist subject." [9]

To be fair, the Royal Thai Government (RTG) has known for some time that the Thai educational system needed a complete overhaul. As far back as 1994, it instituted the Universities Science and Engineering Education Project (USEEP) to attempt to, not only modernize the Thai education system by initiating funding to expand access to education, but also to help reduce shortages of professional and skilled personnel especially in science and engineering. As Rachavarn Kanjanapanyakom and J. Kaya Prpic tell us,

> 'This involved improving and upgrading the standard
> and quality of teaching, as well as rapidly expanding the
> number of science and engineering enrolments in 20
> publicly funded Thai universities (36 faculties).' [10]

While this only focused on the Higher Education sector, the thinking was that you had to start somewhere, and that something like technology would almost certainly start paying for itself sooner rather than later. It was accepted that there were too few modern teaching methodologies, for example the Direct, or Communicative Method, Total Physical Response, kinesthetic but to name a few of the teaching methodologies that are widely accepted as deserving the epithet 'modern', and this stifled any creativity that might otherwise come out of the classroom. Again Kanjanapanyakom and J. Kaya Prpic tell us, 'There appears to be generally little awareness of, or incentive to, develop alternate and student-centred learning teaching methodologies.' [11]

However, these 'progressive' approaches to learning tend to be used in less academic teaching environments and are usually aimed at a younger audience. The main aim of the USEEP project was to improve teaching in Thailand in general, as there were many problems such as poor facilities, unmotivated students, and most important of all, disgruntled teachers. As Rachavarn Kanjanapanyakom and J. Kaya Prpic make clear,

'Many academics shared their feelings of anxiety at
the problem of keeping abreast of rapidly changing trends
in their chosen fields. They expressed their observation
that a number of issues within the Thai University system
compounded this anxiety. These include:

• the limited research infrastructure within the Thai universities, and the consequent dependence on imported information and technology
• a limited supply of current reference material in either Thai or English
• limited funding to provide tutors
• limited workplace experience amongst many of the young academics
• limited industry links
• limited postgraduate and research experience
• changes in the structure of university administration'

Due to the proliferation of international schools, help came in the form of the International Schools Association of Thailand (ISAT), the umbrella organisation which was set up in the same year and which brought a major change in the way schools went about their business, as it's then president, M.L. Pariyada Diskul (also known as Khun Parry), said,

'Back in 1994, the International Schools Association of
Thailand (ISAT) was formed to both promote international
education in Thailand and ensure that standards remain
high.' [12]

Undoubtedly, this has had a major impact on the quality of education, albeit children's education, in Thailand but it is a very welcome change and long overdue. Many of the old teaching methods were replaced by a system that took the child as the central pillar in the classroom. As Khun Parry continues,

> 'All ISAT member schools serve as training centres for
> Thai teachers in line with current educational reforms.
> Within Thai education, there is a much-publicized move
> away from rote learning towards a more child-centred
> approach. Thai teachers are required to observe these
> measures in action to inspire their own teaching. This,
> according to Khun Parry, works well. "It's very popular.
> When they see child-centred education for themselves,
> they get excited as they've only read the theory in a book.
> But when they see it, they can learn and go back to their
> own classrooms and change.' [13]

It is clear then that the increasing number of international schools has ushered in a new era in Thai education as sixty-seven out of the ninety international schools in the country as of 2005 had joined the association. As David Cook, principal of Dulwich International College in Phuket, said at the time, 'The international schools in Bangkok and Thailand must be the largest concentration in the world. The quality of the very good ones is extremely high.' [14] Another prominent member of the international school system, Dr Mark Hensman, principal of Harrow International School said 'We are entering a new phase in international education. There has been rapid growth. It is going to slow down in the next few years which is good because we can now focus on quality rather than numbers.' [15]

Who knows? Maybe the next Einstein is studying right now in a school near you. I wouldn't bet against it.

Chapter Notes:

[1] www.wellofwisdom.com/albert-einstein/0/quotes-author.html

[2] This is a Darwinian idea, which is that statistically, if you gave a million monkeys typewriters and set them to work, they would eventually come up with the complete works of Shakespeare.

[3] Editorials: *Making Thai History: 'A blow to school "tea money" heralds positive change'*, Asiaweek.com
http://www.asiaweek.com/asiaweek/magazine/2000/0512/edit2.html

[4] Coday, Dennis, *Fighting Corruption*, *NCR* staff writer, National Catholic Reporter
http://www.nationalcatholicreporter.org/todaystake/tt100803.htm

[5] Fletcher, Matthew and Gearing, Julian, *'A School for Scandal? Politicians are accused of buying degrees'*, Asiaweek.com
http://www-cgi.cnn.com/ASIANOW/asiaweek/96/0719/nat5.html

[6] Tarver, Nick, *What hope for a superficial education system?*
http://www.ajarn.com/Contris/exwriters/nicktarvernovember2005.htm

[7] Ukosakul, Margaret, *'Face and Politeness in Thai Social Interaction'*,
http://webhost.ua.ac.be/tisp/viewabstract.php?id=791

[8] Sharples, Jennifer, *Famous names have learnt to keep up the old school Thais*
http://www.telegraph.co.uk/global/main.jhtml?xml=/global/2003/03/17/ed schoo217.xml

[9] The English Language Gazette, digital version, Please see Page 2 in September 01, 2010 issue of ODE_ELGazette

[10] Kanjanapanyakom, Rachavarn, and Prpic, J. Kaya, *The Impact of Cultural Values and Norms on Higher Education in Thailand*, Monash

University, Melbourne, Australia, , Kasetsart University, Bangkok, Thailand 1997)

[11] Ibid, Rachavarn, and Prpic

[12] Stoneham, Neil, from *The Bangkok Post*, Learning Post, *THE INTERNATIONAL* EDUCATION BOOM
http://www.bangkokpost.com/education/site2003/cvnv0403.htm

[13] Ibid, Stoneham, Neil

[14] Forestier, Katherine*, Hats off as Thais tread world stage*, South China Morning Post, Monday 11th April, 2005
http://www.classifiedpost.com/jsarticle.php?lcid=HK.EN&artid=3000010 622&arttype=CNEWS&artsection=CED&communitycode

[15] Ibid, quoted in Forestier, Katherine*, Hats off as Thais tread world stage*

(A young woman washes a puppy at "JJ" Market in Bangkok)

Chapter Seven

Thais and Shopping

Shop Till You Drop

As a young teacher, new to the teaching game in Thailand, I would often begin a lesson, especially a new class on a light note, with a few enquiring words and questions to loosen up my charges. The most common answers I believe any teacher in Thailand will tell you to the two questions "What are your hobbies? and, "what do you do in your spare time?" are the two most prolific gerunds in the English language – sleeping and shopping respectively. It is unquestionably the answer that is most often heard in a Thai EFL classroom and goes a long way in illuminating another aspect of the Thai psyche: the great emphasis they put on personal comfort and relaxation.

> *What do you like to do in your free time?'* The young
> assistant manager thinks a while before she answers the
> English teacher during her company's weekly language
> training. After careful consideration she responds:
> *'Sleeping'*. Then she lights up in a smile and adds
> *..and shopping...'* [1]

Actually, there is nothing more telling of Thais as a nation than when visiting a shopping mall on any given Saturday or Sunday and watching the behavior of the local people. This is because shopping in Thailand has become a national institution. The Aussies may have their Australian Rules and cricket, the Japanese, their sushi and Sumo, but the Thais have their Muay Thai and shopping. Any opportunity to visit the nice, air-conditioned coolness of these places is highly prized by the average Thai person. Going to the mall on a Saturday or Sunday is thus as natural/common as eating Jasmine rice for dinner.

It's a curious thing to consider, this Thai love for shopping, given the fact that approximately ninety-five per cent of the population is Buddhist [2], which places great emphasis on impermanence and anti-materialism. So, where does this drive for shopping and, in particular, Western brand goods come from?

One source is undoubtedly connected to the growth of the Internet and cable and satellite channels, which offer up a daily diet of Hollywood movies, slick advertising, and Western lifestyles. Indeed, given that the previous prime minister, Thaksin Shinawatra is a modern-day media mogul with his own media and communication companies, it is not all that surprising the pervasiveness of shopping as a national characteristic for the average Thai.

This trend is set to continue if the latest data on Thailand's youth culture is to be believed. In the interesting article "Thai teens get serious: New market research on the Thailand youth market", we find the following which shows that it is not only prevalent in Thailand but is really an Asian phenomena,

> 'Western culture in the form of MTV and Hollywood movies delivered through satellite TV has been a major influence on youth culture, though MTV features local pop stars and culture to a significant extent. Malaysian Prime Minister Mahathir Mohamad is a stalwart against the inroads of "western culture", seeing it publicly as a threat to "Asian values" but specifically to those of respect for elders and political authority. He even went so far to call Japanese "blondes" for their slavish pursuit of US culture.' [3]

If you look at the general statistics for household spending in Thailand from say, 1997-2004, the amount of money spent in the retail sector shows a percentage increase year-on-year. Moreover, between the years 1999–2003 the average annual income per person rose from 51,384 baht to 54,950 [4] baht, so it is quite clear that Thais have a lot of money to spend, and they generally spent the largest amount of it, on items and activities connected to personal comfort and relaxation and on entertainment in general.

Of course, the main reason why Thais have this extra money to spend is that Thailand is a relatively cheap place to live, and not just because the cost of living is low, but also because the cost of renting apartments, condos, houses etc. is cheap too, relative to other countries.

> 'As accommodation is plentiful and thus relatively
> cheap in Thailand, Thai consumers spend less on
> accommodation than the majority of their western
> counterparts. Accordingly, the larger portion of
> disposable income that may be spent on goods
> increases the country's attractiveness to retailers.' [5]

In fact, in 2001, 40 % of an average Thai person's income was spent on food, beverage, and tobacco as compared to only 26% on accommodation. [6] Compare this with your average European country and you will then see the rather interesting situation that Thais find themselves in: a high disposable income not only makes them attractive to foreign investors with suitable corporate branding, but it also affords them the income to spend on luxury items and gives them the opportunity to indulge in some more personal comfort and relaxation as mentioned above.

What is more surprising though is that almost all Thais, irrespective of age, religion, socio-economic status love shopping. Asian women are, unsurprisingly the most prolific shoppers as Kristian Gotthelf explains,

> 'Here lies a contrast to Asian women who are, in a sense, still
> "shopping purists". They shop not for self-actualization or to
> find a luxury bargain, but to spend and to embrace the
> shopping activity as a social event. Similar to the yuppies of
> the 80's, Asian women are earning and spending, but this
> newly found wealth is part of a newly found freedom as well as
> an economic evolution. In South East Asia more women are
> joining the work force. They are becoming financially
> independent. In the industrialization of many Asian countries is
> the grassroots of a growing freedom for working women.Last
> year a press conference with Thai starlets discussed the
> wonders of the TV Show *"Sex and The City"*. This is a quiet
> women's liberation- Asian style.' [6]

Women play a more than vital role in the retail sector and especially the up-and-coming middle class which, because of Thaksin Shinawatra's ability to quickly pay off Thailand's IMF loans after the Asian Financial Crisis of 1997, have blossomed considerably in the last few years. As Kristian Gotthelf herself says,

> 'Shopping as a life style will continue to grow in Asia, notably among the women from the growing middle class.' [7]

However, whilst Thailand may well have become a hub for shoppers when you think of the available venues in which to pursue such an activity: Emporium, Siam Parragon, Gaysorn Plaza, The World Trade Centre etc., etc it is surprising the level of service that is available in shops, especially department stores. One would think that, with the general liking among the population for shopping and spending money, the quality of service would be generally higher than in, say countries where shopping is not given such a high priority and is, consequently, not so high on one's list of things to do. Sadly, in Thailand, this is often not the case.

Of course, it should be added that I am a European male and so shopping is something that is not second nature to me when compared to say a "shop till you drop" European, or American female, or indeed an Asian female for that matter. Unlike my Asian male cousins, shopping is anathema to me and my hatred of it borders on the pathological with the consequence that the thought of any time spent walking the floors of such buildings leaves me in a cold sweat. As Pam Danziger, president of Unity Marketing says,' When men get stressed, they go to bars, and women go shopping'. Here are some of the reasons why I don't like shopping.

When shopping in Thailand, my pet hate must be sales' assistants following me around the shop, then, when I finally ask them about one of the products, they haven't got a clue about the product they are selling, and I'm left feeling like I'm speaking in Swahili or a little known dialect version of Danish slang. However, when they do have information about the product they are selling, it's often a fib merely to get me to buy the product. A case in point was when I bought a MIDI system in Powerbuy in Emporium a few years ago. The salesman was very kind until I asked him about the guarantee and specifically whether the guarantee covered the whole world, or just Thailand. Quick as a flash he replied "all over the world sir!" Of course I bought the product only to discover, when I got home, that it was only valid in Thailand.

Another time, I bought an external CD burner at PowerBuy only to discover when I got home that (a) it caused a major conflict with my PC and wouldn't work, and (b) the guarantee had began six months earlier and I therefore had only six months remaining. When I took it back to the shop, the sales assistants did the famous head-scratching routine all over again and referred me to the manager, who (a) would not upgrade the guarantee but (b) agreed to change the CD burner for another one. Three further machines later and several months down the line, I still didn't have a CD burner that worked, and the guarantee ran out. When I contacted the Tourist Police, they were not interested in taking up the case unless the amount of money was in excess of 50,000 baht. I still have that burner in a brand new box if anyone's interested!

And here's my personal favourite: when I go into a shop and see something either on sale, or just simply advertised with a copy of the product 'on the shelf' in the store so to speak. This has always meant to me that '*yes, we do actually have the product that you see on the shelf, or in the window, and are happy to get it for you.*' However, in Thailand this is not often the case. There have been many instances where I have said the ubiquitous words that all sales assistants dream of e.g. "I'll take it", only to see the sales assistants invariably rummage round in the back of the store returning ten minutes later to say they *don't* have it. This happens to me regularly and happened to me once when I tried to order some shelves in a *Koncept* store, along with some assorted furniture etc. This also happened to some friends of mine who also said "I'll take it" to a 55,000 baht Plasma TV only to find it was out of stock in *Big C* and also in *Carrefour*. I could bombard you with hundreds more examples, but the fact is Thai people are not all that hot when it comes to the finer points of supply chain management styles and often forget to keep a semblance of stock control.

I have often asked myself whether it's even possible to make a profit with these kinds of business practices. Add to this the fact that there are often three times as many sales assistants as customers in many stores, and the answer would have to be a resounding 'no!' But they do, and the statistics for the growth of foreign stores in Thailand is growing every year. Stores like *Tesco Lotus*, *Carrefour*, *Big C*, and *Makro* are everywhere and look

90

likely to continue to do so. In 2003 alone, these four companies had a combined total of 130 stores in Thailand, either as supermarkets or hypermarkets with a typical floor space of approximately 6,000 square metres.[8]

Yet another bizarre incidence occurred when I was in a large *Carrefour* hypermarket and wanted to return a brake pedal lock for a car. I had mistakenly bought the manual version when I needed the automatic one. No problem, until I realized that in order to get a refund on this item, I first had to buy *another* one e.g. I had to buy another brake pedal lock *first*. This is all very well if the item is only 1,200 baht, as the pedal lock was, but what if it had been the 55,000 baht TV? Apparently, the same procedure is followed much to my amazement!

Ok, I am obviously giving a very male perspective here, but for all my hatred of shopping and branded clothing items, one thing is certain. I am surrounded by a nation of enthusiastic shoppers. Napoleon famously said of the country I grew up in, 'England is a nation of shopkeepers' [9]. If he were alive today, one wonders what he would make of the Thais? No doubt he would have been impressed with the way they are so able to organise local markets as you can find one almost on every street corner, ok not quite, but it often seems like it as they are pretty much everywhere.

In reality, you don't have to go very far to find a market open somewhere in Thailand. They are almost like the car boot sales so loved by English people in the eighties and garage sales that the Americans have always loved. In these markets, you will find the true entrepreneurial spirit of the Thai. People will stand for hours at a time without seemingly selling anything and will return again the next day with a big smile and a renewed sense of optimism.

The most popular markets are Chatuchack (or *Talad JJ* as it is more commonly known), [10] which is only open at the weekends and Fridays. Here it will take you three or four hours to get all the way around and you can buy anything from a Thai dog (known as a *Bang Gaeow*) to a plant or anything else for the home and garden. Another is called Pratunam Market, which is located in the center of Bangkok and is usually bustling with people morning, noon and night. Just about anything and everything is on sale here but it is especially known for clothes. Be prepared to wade in and out of crowds though as it is rarely quiet. Oh, and if you find it too hot to shop in an outdoor market in the heat of the day don't forget the Suan Loom Night Bazaar next to the entrance to Silom Road

Shopping then for the Thais is a more than just acquiring new possessions although of course new possessions are highly prized. It is a way of sharing an experience with someone special, be it your mother, wife, husband or brother. It is a way of enjoying the finer things in life and an escape from the humdrum existence, the dreariness of ordinary life, the overbearing humidity, the uncertainty of the tropical climate, and one thing is for sure - it is unlikely to change any time soon.

Thailand may well be going through a period of political instability. Add to that the crisis in the financial markets with the Credit Crunch and the slowing down of world economies because of the problems with money being frozen with the Sub Prime Mortgages in the USA. However, that all being said, Thailand is unlikely to stop shopping. As Sujintana Hemtasilpa concludes,

> 'No matter what form the next government takes
> or what its policies will be, Thai people are unlikely
> to lose their zeal for shopping, even if economic
> growth slows in the short term.' [11]

Ok, that's the shopping done. Now time for some sleep!

Chapter Notes:

[1] *The Asian Women's Shopping Experience: New research from Thailand*, June 20, (2003)
http://www.asiamarketresearch.com/news/000309.htm

[2] Pricewaterhouse Coopers, Thailand Retail Trade Figures, in *From Beijing to Budapest: New Retail & Consumer Growth Dynamics in Transitional Economies,* http://www.pwc.com/extweb/pwcpublications.nsf/docid/8fea5f592d0a712 c80256f1c00547442

[3] *Thai teens get serious: New market research on the Thailand youth market,* http://www.asiamarketresearch.com/news/000258.htm

[4] Op Cit. Pricewaterhouse Coopers

[5] Ibid, Pricewaterhouse Coopers

[6] Ibid, Pricewaterhouse Coopers

[7] Op Cit, *The Asian Women's Shopping Experience*

[8] Op Cit, Pricewaterhouse Coopers

[9] Bonaparte, Napoleon, "A Nation of Shopkeepers" ("L'Angleterre est une nation de boutiquiers") is a disparaging remark supposedly used by Napoleon to describe the United Kingdom as unfit for war against France. The phrase was not, however, original. Napoleon could have found it in *The Wealth of Nations* (1776) by Adam Smith, who wrote:

"To found a great empire for the sole purpose of raising up a people of customers may at first sight appear a project fit only for a nation of shopkeepers. It is, however, a project altogether unfit for a nation of shopkeepers; but extremely fit for a nation whose government is influenced by shopkeepers." http://en.wikipedia.org/wiki/Nation_of_shopkeepers

[10] Suriyakham, Sippakon, *Bangkok shopping bargains,* http://www.smarttravelasia.com/bangkokshop.htm

[11] Hemtasilpa, Sujintana, *Consuming With a Difference* http://www.bangkokpost.net/ecoreviewye2004/retailing.html

(Typically funny mispelt Thai menu)

Chapter Eight

Thais and Wordplay

The Butterfly Effect

One thing that always struck me right from my first days in the Thai kingdom is the people here love playing with words every bit much as the people in the land where I was brought up – England. In fact, the first word or phrase that I learnt in Thailand (after the ubiquitous *Sawasdee crap* greeting) was *poot len*, which means quite literally "speak play". Indeed, I constantly marvel at the Thai love of word play, so intrinsic is it to their culture and which very much illuminates aspects of them as a race of people. [1]

One early example of this that sticks out was when I was teaching in my first job in Siam Square. I had been teaching a group of elementary students, (probably because the Director of Studies wouldn't let me near a higher level class for fear that I might confuse them owing mainly to my lack of any discernible teaching experience at that time.) A student gave an answer to a question of which I don't remember exactly, but then burst into peals of laughter along with the rest of the class. Surprised, I asked what it was I had said that was funny. The student explained thus utilizing the phrase *poot len* meaning she had been having a joke or a laugh with me (or should that have been at my expense?) Anyway, there have been innumerable instances where such a thing has occurred over the many years I have since been teaching, and they go a long way to highlighting the Thai penchant for playing around with language.

Actually, this is not an unusual occurrence amongst communities of language users. It has been known for a long time the way people will use language in a particular way that appeals to and indeed creates a specific tone, register, or ambience for the recipients of the language. You only have to think of the ways young children will develop their own language that their parents cannot understand to get a sense of this. Teens often do this too and develop a form of slang that only the members of their group can understand and identifies them as such. Ludvig Wittgenstein's theory of 'language-games' develops this idea considerably with his view on the ways communities of language users play a particular language-game. Like the rules of a game, chess, cricket, football, Wittgenstein argued, these rules for the use of ordinary language are neither right nor wrong, neither true nor false: they are merely useful for the particular applications in which we apply them. The members of any community—accountants, college students, or musicians, for example—develop ways of speaking that serve their needs as a group, and these constitute the language-game. [2]

For me, one of the funniest experiences of language I have had was when I was a teacher in a relatively new class of students. I believe it was only the second or third class of this particular course. I was there at the start of the class waxing lyrical about something like homework or such thing and in walks this stunning young lady called Jim (yes, a bit of a mismatch, but Thais do like to give themselves nicknames) and sits down. As she is new, I ask her to introduce herself to everybody. She is a bit nervous, so I try to help by introducing myself and the other students first. Eventually, and somewhat gingerly, she offers the following:

'Hello, my name is Supaporn, but you can call me Jim'

Ok so far, so I reply,

'Nice to meet you Jim. So, tell us a little bit about youself. For example, what do you want to do when you graduate?'

Quick as a flash she replies,

'Sir, I would like to be an air *hostage*!'

Speckles of laughter descend on the room. I try to regain some sense of order and try to rescue Jim.

'So, tell us Jim. This sounds like an exciting job. What would you have to do in this job?'

With an angelic smile on her face that could have made you think she was Mother Teresa's daughter, she replies,

'I would have to *service* the passengers sir.'

It should be said that, although the Thai language has a wonderful ability to render itself open to being presented in funny ways, as we've seen, it's also worth remembering what I said before (in Chapter Five) that Thais like a fun, relaxed environment to dwell in, and this also helps to provide a *mileu* for having fun in communication, too. What better way to foster a nice atmosphere than to play around with words and build harmonious relationships at the same time?

Moreover, Thai is known as a high context language and, as I said before, great care is taken to promote a pleasant environment. As J. Kaya Prpic and Rachavarn Kanjanapanyakom tell us, there is an unusual number of personal pronouns in Thai which are used to embed and solidify relationships,

> 'The concept of high context communication is further emphasized in Thai language itself, which stresses the importance of social harmony. Thai pronouns are a critical way in which Thai people position themselves in relationships. Whereas English speakers have only one alternative available for 'I' and 'you', the Thai language offers 17 forms of the first pronoun and up to 19 forms of the second pronoun. Which pronoun is used depends on the relative politeness, intimacy, and status of those involved in the conversation.' [3]

The language is not only funny because of the way it is used, but also because of its underlying structure. There are many reasons for this. The first is that Thais like to assign arbitrary terms for words, which don't refer to the object being described. Take the following word for butterfly in Thai – '*pee seua*', literally "ghost shirt". The imagery here is marvelous as a butterfly with outstretched wings could easily be imagined to be a ghost moving with a shirt flapping in the wind (much like the early ghost stories in Victorian Gothic literature that feature drawings of white sheets seemingly floating in darkened bedrooms). Another example is '*kee dao*' which means in general "your smelly armpit" but can also refer to a "smelly turtle" Similarly, "poo maa" which is a type of crab can also literally mean "crab horse" when translated verbatim. And my favourite –

tawng rawng, which means "singing stomach" (used when you are hungry and your stomach is rumbling) This shows some of the ways in which Thai has mixture of unusual and funny linguistic turns.

Another reason is that Thais add compounds together that are often so literal, that they appear in funny combinations. Here is an example – *kon fao pratoo* - which literally translated means – 'person' 'light' 'door'. Can you guess what this person does for a living? The answer is open doors and shine torches in cinemas, what in English used to be called an 'usher' or 'usherette' (female). Another example is 'maewfawbaahn' which I'll let others explain,

> 'In Thai, the word 'cat' is 'maew', the word 'watch'
> (in the sense of 'to watch over') is 'faw', and the word
> for 'house' is 'baan'. The word for 'watch cat' (like a
> watchdog) is the compound 'maewfawbaahn' – literally,
> 'catwatchhouse'. [4]

Another interesting aspect of compounding in the Thai language can be found in the fact that according to the Guinness Book of Records the formal Thai word for Bangkok has the longest place name at one hundred and seventy-seven characters.

> Krung-thep-maha-nakorn-boworn-ratana-kosin-mahintar
> -ayudhya-amaha-dilok-pop-nopa-ratana-rajthani-burirom
> -udom-rajniwes-mahasat-arn-amorn-pimarn-avatar-satit
> -sakattiya-visanukam. [5]

This is actually often misunderstood as most kiwis will tell you that in fact the place, which officially has the longest place name according to the Guinness Book of Records, is a hill near Porangahau, Hawkes Bay, which is spelt with either 85 or 92 letters depending on how you choose to spell it.

> Taumatawhakatangihangakoauauotamateaturipukaka
> pikimaunga horonukupokaiwhenuakitanatahu [6]

It is interesting to ask not only *how* Thai has developed this funny linguistic characteristic, but also *why*? In the German language, we also find a lot of compound words, but is not the least bit funny at all, and has a rather 'hard on the ear', finality about it when such words are pronounced. Equally, English has a remarkable ability to make compound words without all this comic effect as Bill Bryson explains in his wonderful *Mother Tongue*,

> "Finally, but no less importantly, English possesses the ability to make new words by fusing compounds – *airport, seashore, footwear, wristwatch, landmark, flowerpot*, and so on almost endlessly. All Indo-European languages have the capacity to form compounds. Indeed German and Dutch do it, one might say, to excess. But English does it more neatly than most other languages, eschewing the choking word chains that bedevil other Germanic languages and employing the nifty refinement of making the elements reversible, so that we can distinguish between a houseboat and a boat house between basketwork and a workbasket, between a casebook and a bookcase. Other languages lack this facility." [7]

It is clear then that Thai tends to focus on a meaning that is in a way, *aslant* or *askew* to the literal meaning, and that other languages e.g. German and English, whilst employing the same linguistic device, compounding, find more practical benefits to it use.

It may well also be added that European languages have less use for such words or their combinations that do not directly relate, ostensively, to the object they represent. In the song 'Supercalifragilisticexpialidocious' from the Musical 'Mary Poppins' we get the following very British advice about the use of words,

> 'That's not a word'
> Course it's a word. And, unless I am very much mistaken
> I think it's going to prove a rather useful one.
> When trying to express oneself,
> it's frankly quite absurd,
> to leaf through lengthy lexicons,
> to find the perfect word.
> A little spontaneity keeps conversation keen,
> you need to find a way to say precisely what you mean'.[8]

This last example is the one most Thais aspire to considering it unimportant to be too literal with meaning.

Another aspect of Thai that has a certain lyrical quality to it can be found in the various tongue twisters that can be found, as the following will demonstrate,

'Chao gin pad fuck,
Yen gin fuck pad,
Chaam keeow quam chao,
Chaam khao quan come.' [9]

Try saying that after a brace of beer *Changs* and a spicy *Tom Yam Goong* soup. It literally means "morning eat pumpkin, evening eat pumpkin, green bowl turn over morning, white bowl turn over evening" Or for an easier to understand form, "pumpkins are eaten in the morning and pumpkins are eaten in the evening. Green bowls are turned over in the morning, and white bowls are turned over in the evening."

This is probably closest linguistically to the English tongue twister,

'Peter Piper picked a peck of pickled peppers;
A peck of pickled peppers Peter Piper picked;
If Peter Piper picked a peck of pickled peppers,
Where's the peck of pickled peppers Peter Piper picked?' [10]

Yet another example is the following,

'*Mai mai mai* ' which can mean (with the correct tones), 'The silk is not new'. I was once mildly and jokingly berated by a student in an elevator who asked me somewhat ironically, why I always wanted to eat a 'knee' for lunch? I had of course mistaken the correct tone of "khao" which has five equally different tones, and yes, one of which means "knee", so in fact I had been saying '*Pom yak gin khao*' thinking it meant "I want to eat some rice" but in fact was saying "I want to eat (someone's) knee!"

But my favourite aspects of the funniness of Thai language has to do with the often needed necessity for translating words from Thai into English, and it here that again the unwitting foreigner comes across the unbearably funny spelling of the Thais.

When I first came to Thailand I would read the funny translations on the various menus and wonder who must've been the person who had been given the somewhat onerous task of translating all the various dishes into English? Here are just a few of the many favourites that I have seen on Thai menus and collected over the years,

- Bang Lump Poo
- Fried milk
- Squid in Love
- Green curry with drunken chicken
- Sticky and Embroiled rice
- Crab in coco's nuts
- Big crap in pot
- Sweet coriander with Grilled surgeon
- Roast duck let loose
- Chicken girl with bra zil leaf

I once saw this sign displayed outside a Bangkok *ran ahan,* restaurant,

'Our aberrant atmosphere wound lead in a world in which all senses are contented. This is Restaurant "Big Crap"! Our craps are biggest in Asian! A restaurant "Big Crap" is from the type new and bars with modern design feature quality. A restaurant with flair to the good cookhouse and advertant hand-picked wines. We do not make compromises with the quality that wound not offer. We think that the success obscures itself in attitude to the detail and its good use. We aim therefore to offer only that which will fulfill your expectations to you for quality and a prestige. The fanciers to the good cookhouse will discover a special in each dish cook by our actor culinarist Somchai Ekkachart that had completed one from the most prestigious colleges in England, as well as had a diploma with the brand – "Le Cordon Bleu" that is guarantor for excellent knowing and command in the traditional Thai kitchen. Somchai Ekkachart has

102

been an alma mater at the european cookery school and has specialized in fishy restaurants, that are one from the most known in England.'

But if you think that mishaps with the Thai language can only happen to Thais, you'd be wrong. Here is just one of the many examples where farangs try to use the local language with disastrous consequences, in this case, me. The following is an experience I had when I had not been in Thailand all that long. I was working for a company on Wireless Road in the heart of Bangkok. I had gone to the bathroom to take a leak, and when I returned someone had put a note on my desk asking me to go and see a Thai member of staff. Curious, and wanting to practice my limited Thai with her, I walked up to her desk and, in my best Thai, tried to say 'did you want me?' which I thought in Thai was *'khun ow pom mai?'*

She was in hysterics for five minutes, during which a crowd of more Thai staff had gathered around to see what was going on. When she managed to pull herself together, after almost being on the floor with laughter, she asked me to repeat it, so I did. Now the entire crowd was in hysterics. When they had all returned to normality, I asked them for the real translation of what I just said - 'Do you want me (sexually)?'

I remember this one from a student after a particularly long and difficult course where I had felt a complete failure in getting my message across to the students. On his way out the door, one student turned around and said, with complete sincerity and a big smile on his face, 'Goodbye. Come to see us when you are interesting!'

Chapter Notes:

[1] The word *'len'* is used a lot in Thai and, other than the usual uses for the translation into 'play' (football, golf and the other normal, sporting uses) it is used to denote some sense of playing around with something like a word e.g. *'gin len'* which means 'play eating' although in terms of general meaning, this is something similar in English to snacking. www.enjoythaifood/thaimeals.php

[2] Wittgenstein, Ludvig, *Tractatus Logico Philosophicus*, 6.1, Routledge Classics, Second edition (September 1, 2001)

[3] Kanjanapanyakom, Rachavarn, and Prpic, J. Kaya, *The Impact of Cultural Values and Norms on Higher Education in Thailand*, Monash University, Melbourne, Australia, Kasetsart University, Bangkok, Thailand (1997)

[4] *An Introduction to Language*, First Canadian Edition, (1997), Harcourt Brace, Canada

[5] *Thailand Has World's Longest Place Name*
http://www.fun-with-words.com/longest_place_names.html

[6] Ibid

[7] Bryson, Bill, *Mother Tongue*, Penguin Books, (1991)

[8] *Funny Language*, http://www.chiangmai-chiangrai.com/funny_language.html

[9] http://www. Thai-language.com/id/589866

[10] Mother Goose, *Peter Piper picked a peck of pickled peppers* http://www.amherst.edu/~rjyanco94/literature/mothergoose/rhymes/peterp iperpickedapeckofpickledpeppers.html

(A colourful Songkran float makes its way through a Bangkok Street)

Chapter Nine

Thais and Their Customs

Any Old Wet Wednesday

It's really not surprising that a lot of Thai festivals involve water of some kind or another. This is because it is, like Samuel Taylor Coleridge says, 'water, water everywhere but not a drop to drink'. [1] Consider Thailand's ubiquitous canals, the fact that most of its eastern and southern border is surrounded by the Gulf of Thailand, the fact also that an extremely large river called the Chao Phraya runs through its capital city, and you only begin to get an idea of the role that water of every kind plays in Thai life.

It is also a well-known adage that you can judge a race by their customs, and nowhere is this more true than in Thailand. Thai people have many unique customs and festivals, and they really do show another dimension to their collectivist nature. Moreover, because Thai society is, as we saw in Chapter Two, very hierarchical in nature, Thais themselves place great emphasis on their customs, which reflect this hierarchy. There are many local and national festivals but there are two main ones: perhaps the most colourful of these festivals, and also the best known, is Songkran.

Songkran

The Songkran festival, which is also the Thai New Year, can be translated literally as "the passing of", as Songkran marks the beginning of the solar calendar. It usually occurs at the end of the second week of April although actual dates vary from region to region according to the lunar cycle. During the holiday period people visit shrines and pour water over a range of Buddhist statues to bring good fortune. The family sprinkling scented water from silver bowls on a Buddha image is a ritual practiced by all Thais in on the third day of Songkran, known as *Wan Payawan*.

However, one way that this festival shows or underpins the innate hierarchy of Thai life is in the way, for example, young students are shown the real meaning behind Songkran. In true Thai tradition, early in the morning, a daughter or son will sprinkle water over the hands of his or her parents in order to show respect thus underpinning a very Thai notion that the young must pay respect to their elders. A small amount of water can also be poured over the shoulders as a sign of respect. The person receiving the water will sometimes recite a Buddhist incantation. But perhaps the most important aspect of this festival is the variety of ways in which water is used. It is symbolic as the quintessential element of the festival.

> 'Water is central to Songkran. Buddha images are
> washed with lustral water, while the whole house is
> given an especially thorough cleaning. The idea is to
> start the New Year fresh and clean, both in body and
> spirit. Most noticeably to the casual visitor, though,
> Thais also lay in wait outside to douse each other
> (and any passing visitor) with water. The custom of
> throwing water is probably just an exuberant spill
> over of the tradition of pouring lustral water over the
> hands of monks and respected elders. More basically,
> the return of water to the parched soil is an
> expression of hope and anticipation, an invitation to
> the cooling, life-giving rainy season to come.' [2]

At this time, the whole country appears to grind to a halt, and getting around on the main arterial roads is nigh on impossible as there are huge numbers of pick up trucks, mini bus vans, motorcycles, indeed any form of transport can and will be used to carry revelers on the highways in order that those on board can throw water onto others to show respect. You have to remember too that this festival takes place at the hottest time of the year in Thailand and so for most people, this is a welcome way to cool down.

In addition to the transfer of water onto another person, there is a white powder like paste, which is usually daubed onto the face or neck. Again, this shows the way rank is important as the elders usually put the white paste on the faces of young people.

'As part of the water sprinkling, water splashing and string tying rites, you may also encounter a person with a small silver bowl filled with a white powder or pasty substance. This is one of the oldest Songkran traditions. The white paste is a sign of protection and promises to ward off evil. The person with the paste is often older and he or she applies the paste to various parts of the face, neck and torso of others. One is expected to leave this paste on until it washes off of its own accord, and while there is a tendency to shy away from this paste because it looks like it might ruin the clothes, it is water soluble and will not harm materials.' [3]

But of course the festival has undergone a host of changes over the years and, nowadays, it tends to be enjoyed a lot more by the working class than by the middle class or those with money. Part of the reason for this is the Thai aversion to being out in hot weather for any length of time. Another reason is that Thais generally value their appearance and being drenched in water and covered in sticky, white powder for any length of time does little for one's self esteem. Yet another reason is that, whereas in the past, the whole festival used to be a very sedate affair, very calm and respectful whereby people would walk gently up to you and ask permission before demurely pouring water over some neutral part of your body, it has at times become a bit rowdy.

Nowadays, gangs of Thai youths, already through their third or fourth beer Chang approach you and, with the aid of large super powerful water pistols, blast you in the face with water then proceed to daub unwitting tourists with the said white paint. As the German actors used to say in the old war films 'resistance is futile'. There have been worrying reports too that the powder may find its way to less neutral parts of the body, especially where young, pretty girls are concerned, but of course it doesn't matter where you are when you have a carnival atmosphere, copious amounts of booze and plenty of free time, these things are almost always bound to happen.

On a personal note, a friend and former colleague who had been a teacher here for a number of years was cutting through Patpong Soi 2 in Bangkok a few years ago on the second day of a Songkran festival when he was confronted by a group of young beer guzzling Thai males. As he was on his way to an important meeting, he was dressed in a suit and tie and was, to all intents and purposes, 'dressed to the nines'. What happened you may ask? Well, at first the Thai males were reasonably polite telling him that all who wanted to pass through the soi had first to allow themselves to be sprinkled with some water and then the usual daubing of white powder. When my friend explained in his best Thai that he was wearing his best clothes and on his way to an important meeting (*mee prajoom sam khan*) there was a quick scrum-like conflab amongst the Thais. However, a few seconds later they turned around and said that he must still have the water and sticky powder. When they approached him, he naturally tried to defend himself and punches were thrown from the Thais. My friend ended up in the hospital with minor bruises. Of course, this is a very rare incident because, by and large, the festival is a very happy affair where the young and old, foreign and local, rich and poor all mingle together in a happy environment.

Another worrying trend is the amount of road related deaths at this time of year. In 2003, 547 people were killed on the roads and a further 35,891 were injured or hospitalized. There were 902 casualties during New Year 2004 and 840 during Songkran 2005, more than the highly publicised 652 deaths in the US attack on Iraq and the 814 deaths from Sars worldwide. [4]

This prompted Tairjing Siripanich, director of the Public Health Ministry's medical institute for accident and disaster prevention to say the following,

> 'Forty people die from road accidents each day in
> Thailand. During Songkran it doubles or triples.
> These are purposeless deaths." He said people were
> more afraid of Sars or bird flu because they thought
> accidents would never happen to them, or if so only
> by bad luck. "In fact it's not a matter of luck: people
> can protect themselves from road accidents.' [5]

Loy Kratong Day

Another festival of note is Loy Kratong Day. This festival is usually held on the first full moon day of November. Like it's sister, Songkran, it involves water as a form of paying respect, this time to the river or *Mae Naam*, down at the banks of the Chao Phraya river if you happen to be in Bangkok, or pretty much any stretch of water in the country if you don't. The idea behind this particular festival is principally to thank the God of the river for providing the water that has so many uses for the city. Unfortunately, nowadays, the grand irony is that in thanking the river they are invariably polluting it with their non- biodegradable foam kratongs and whatnot.

You will most likely hear schoolchildren singing a very traditional song thus,

> 'On the full moon day of the 12th lunar month
> Water overflows the banks
> All of us, both boys and girls
> Will have fun together on Loi Gratong Day!
> Loi, Loi Gratong...Loi, Loi Gratong
> When we've floated our gratongs
> We'll ask Nawng Gaew to come out and
> dance the ramwong
> Dance the ramwong on Loi Gratong Day
> Dance the ramwong on Loi Gratong Day
> Making merit will bring us happiness
> Making merit will bring us happiness' [6]

From there, they will prepare their kratongs (*floating baskets*) – small, inflatable boats made traditionally from a banana tree or Spider Lily plant and other biodegradable materials, though nowadays mostly from Styrofoam or polystyrene. The ceremony is not an especially elaborate one with incense and candles being lit and the kratong pushed gently away from the water bank. Not unlike the blowing out of candles for a bithday party, a wish is then made, sometimes with the hands being raised in a traditional Thai 'wai', as the kratong floats, wending its way away to meet the current of the river. According to one Thai custom, people must keep their eyes on their kratong until it has completely drifted out of sight as there is a strong belief that the longer the candle remains burning, the better the next year will be.

Another tradition related to this festival is to do with romance. Young Thai boyfriends and girlfriends will go down to the river or canal and float their kratongs together. The reason for this is primarily to thank the river goddess, but also to see if the young lovers are compatible or not. If the two kratongs start out together but then go off in different directions, then it is a sure signs that the relationship will not last the test of time, and that they will soon separate. If the kratongs go along steadily for a time, diverge, then reconnect with each other, then the relationship will be difficult but it will survive intact. If the two kratongs diverge sharply at the beginning and do not reconnect, it is apparently a sure sign that the relationship will end very soon.

My first memorable experience of this began only a few days after I had arrived in 1997. I had been invited to go to a ceremony held at the edge of a river to sail my kratong. Everything was going fine, and I had a nice new group of students who, although I was very much a greenhorn, hung on every word I said as if I was a maharishi come to bring divine teachings.

As instructed I had gone to one of the many kratong sellers, which adorned both sides of the road, Phra Athit Road, behind Banglamphu. I tried valiantly to use my newly acquired Thai, which really consisted of two phrases (1) *tao rai crap*? Which means '*How much is that please*? and, (2) *load noi dai ma crap*? - *Can you reduce the price*? Unsurprisingly, I wasn't able to negotiate a cheap price, but then how would I, when I had yet to learn numbers like 100, 200, 250, etc., etc. The kratong I ended up with was a cross between a 2nd World War U-boat and a wreath for someone recently departed. I duly met my students at the river's edge and they goaded me to float my kratong. I did as asked and my kratong promptly sank without a trace.

Chapter Notes:

[1] Coleridge, Samuel Taylor, *The Rime of the Ancient Mariner*, published by: Dover Publications Inc. paperback 28 February, (1971) - text of the 1798 version.
http://en.wikipedia.org/wiki/The_Rime_of_the_Ancient_Mariner

[2] http://www.phuketmagazine.com/Culture/major_thai_festivals.html

[3] http://www.chiangmai-chiangrai.com/rites_of_songkran.html

[4] *Horriffic Death Toll on Thai roads during Songkran*
http://meanderon.blogspot.com/2006/04/horrific-death-toll-on-thai-roads.html

[5] *Tryst With Death,*
http://www.thailandqa.com/forum/showthread.php?t=3697

[6] http://www.geocities.com/siamsmile365/loigratong1/loigratong1.htm

(A typical street restaurant on Silom Road selling delicious Thai food.)

Chapter Ten

Thais and Food

Some Like it Hot!

Just as Winston Churchill famously said that 'the civilisation of a society can be judged by the way it treats its prisoners' [1] equally, it is a well-known fact that a nation's cuisine reflects something about the people who create and eat it. It is in this sense that Thailand is no exception. As most people know, in terms of taste, Thai food can be separated into four distinct kinds: salty, spicy, sweet and sour. Of course, the accepted wisdom is that all Thai food is hot, and there are considerable grounds for that belief especially given that the Thai monicker for chillis is *Prik Kee noo,* which literally means 'shit hot'. The combination of lime and vinegar is used to draw heat from the chilies. This infuses the whole dish with the flavor and heat of the chili and also goes a long way in encouraging the myth that all Thais like spicy food, which of course is not true.

Personally, before I came to Thailand, I had never been too fond of hot and spicy food. My experience of this was mostly from the hot Indian curries, the *dahls*, the *vindaloos*, and the *Chicken Tikka Masalas* consumed on a Friday night after several beers in my local English pub. When I came to Thailand all that changed and now there's nothing I like to see more than a table full of Thai dishes. Back then, because I didn't like the hot, spicy food that is so ubiquitous in Thailand, I more often than not used to settle for the sweeter, more savoury Thai dishes. The best examples of this are found in curry or soup dishes like *Tom Kha Gai* or the famous green curry – *Geng Keeow Waan Gai,* which is a thick, creamy soup or curry. Its principal ingredient is coconut milk, which gives it its distinctly sweet flavour.

Sourness is another flavor distinctive of Thai cuisine, and it mostly comes from the use of citrus fruits such as lime juice. Combining such a variety of all these taste sensations is what makes this cuisine so unique and full of flavour. And according to ancient Chinese medicine, sweet, salty, spicy, bitter, and sour tastes correspond to the five essential elements needed by the human body. Likewise, the sour – *preeow* - category is best illustrated with what is perhaps the most famous dish in all of Thailand – *Tom yam goong*. This dish is a hot spicy soup and has at its core lemongrass, galangal and kaffir lime leaves, which, along with lime, give it its uniquely sour taste. Here's how one commentator describes the relationship,

> 'The foundation of the Thai culinary vocabulary
> consists of varying degrees of hot, sour, sweet and
> salty. Hot comes from a wide variety of fresh and
> dried chilies. Sour includes citrus, tamarind and
> vinegar. Sweet comes from sugar including palm
> sugar. Salty comes from sea salt and fish sauce.
> Built upon this foundation are a staccato of herbs,
> aromatics and spices that lend the distinctive
> character and complexity to specific Thai dishes.
> Principle herbs are coriander, basil in a variety
> of distinctive forms, and, to a lesser degree, mint.
> (Mint is much more prominent in Vietnamese
> cooking.) Aromatics include lemongrass, garlic,
> shallots, ginger, galangal and kaffir lime.' [2]

Geography also plays its part in the variety of Thai food. Again, Thai food can be separated into four distinct regions: Central Thailand, the North of Thailand, The Northeast, also known as Issan, and the South of Thailand. Together, they make up the great range and diversity of flavours that is uniquely Thai. It is interesting to note too, how well Thai food compares with other countries in Asia. For my money, Thai food is by far the best in Asia when you consider factors like variety, cost, availability, and the sheer pride that Thai people have for it. Having travelled in Asia, I can say that, for me, the worst, or should I say, the most vapid food in this region is the food from Cambodia and tastes like someone's old socks, which had been boiled in yesterday's bath water. Japanese food is of course world famous for it's general standards of cuisine and variety, but it is considerably more expensive, and, for that very reason is far less accessible than Thai food.

In Central Thailand, the local food is, as usual, hot, salty, sweet and sour and, because it has many great rivers that converge in this delta, making it a fertile plain for rice growing, there are many dishes which reflect this relationship with water. Not only is *Tom yum goong* (shrimp soup with lemon grass) a favorite dish, but there are many others, which also show this connection with the river or water.

Favorite and or famous dishes of the Central Plains include, *Nam Prik* chili paste dip made with shrimp paste *(kapee)* which is eaten with seasonal vegetables i.e. morning glory, makok, and cha-om. Salads (*yam*) mixed with fresh kaffir lime leaves, lemongrass and herbs. Curry is made with a paste of spicy Thai chilies, onions, garlic, galangal, lemongrass, coriander roots, kaffir lime peel, and *kapee.* Eggs are an all day, every day food including omelettes (*Kai Jeow)* stuffed with minced pork and fried eggs sunny-side up on top of basil stir-fried chicken. The Central Plains version of the Issan salad *som tam* is sweeter, more sour, and includes the addition of ground peanuts influenced by the King's palace kitchens *Khao Chae*, a cooling summertime rice dish. Prepared dishes usually contain many condiments and dried spices. [3]

In the North of Thailand, the food is mild or hot, salty and sour, but almost never sweet. Because the land is mostly jungle-covered mountains and valleys, there are plenty of vegetables and fruits that can grow in cooler mountain areas: they include strawberries, apples, and carrots. Historically this area is famous for sticky rice (glutinous rice), which is served with steamed vegetables, *nam phrik oong*, soups and Northern-style curries are common. The North is also well known for *naem*, a sour sausage made of fermented minced pork, wrapped and steamed in banana leaf.

The Northeast (Issan) region also has its own style of preparing and cooking Thai food. Perhaps the most famous recipes here are *Pla ra, pla som*, and *pla daek,* which are the most distinctive features of Issan food. *Pla ra* seasons curry (*Pla ra* is the Issan equivalent of fish sauce) Chili pastes known as *jaew* - chilies, garlic, salt, *'pla ra'* and lime juice. However, people from this region also have a reputation for eating almost anything for protein including frogs, birds, snakes, and even insects. Arguably the most famous dish is again *som tam*, a spicy green papaya salad, sticky rice served in small baskets called *gktratip*, rolled into a ball and eaten with grilled chicken and *naem*, the slightly fermented sausage with a slight sour taste. [4]

In the South of Thailand, there is an abundance of coconut trees and seafood. Food in the South is renowned for being strong in taste - very hot, salty and sour. Spicy curries are eaten every day, especially coconut curry and sour curry. Generally Southerners eat more fish than meat because they reside close to the sea. The most common dipping sauce or paste is *nam phrik kapee* (also called *nam chuke*) eaten with raw vegetables and crispy fried fish. This dipping sauce is prepared with the best quality shrimp paste (*kapee or kuey*), fresh chilies (*prik kee noo*), and fresh limejuice. [5]

However, there are some types of food eaten in Thailand, which are decidedly less tempting and belong more to game shows like *Fear Factor*. In markets that sell Isaan food, it is possible to eat bugs like scorpions, grasshoppers, larva, beetles and even the occasional dog. This latter urban treat is probably connected to the influence of Chinese culinary traditions although it is a fact that until 1984, in China at least, it was actually illegal to keep a dog as a pet. These days, many Thai farmers are making more by harvesting lice than rice, and indeed now some Bangkok residents enjoy nothing more than to delve into a plateful of bugs: canned grasshoppers, locusts, water beetles, crickets, silkworm pupae and ant eggs are all available at the supermarket should this be your particular poison. It is therefore not that surprising to note that Bangkok residents think of bugs as a healthy, low-calorie treat.

Equally, less tempting for me personally, although hugely popular, is the durian fruit famed for its smell, which is a mixture of sweaty laundry and sour milk. Yet, ask your average Thai, and he or she will proudly say it's the most delicious tasting fruit ever. Unsurprisingly, it's known by the Thais as 'The King of the Fruits'.

> 'The fruit called durian is famous for its smell when it
> is ripe. Durians are often forbidden in public places
> such as Thai hotels. This is due to the strong smell of the
> durian, which persists even if the fruit has been moved
> to another place. One thing is for sure, nobody can steal
> a durian. Due to the smell, it is impossible to hide it!'[6]

For me, whatever your palette, what is remarkable about Thai food is that, although there is a well-established tradition of eating outside the home, ask the average girl in the street, let's call her Navaporn, and not only will she be able to tell you how to cook particular Thai dishes, but she'll be able to cook the dish herself without any problems and with the minimum of fuss. How can this be so when almost everyone eats out? Where could Navaporn have learnt the skills to make these incredible dishes? Is there some collective will, some sense of shared knowledge or history that enables all Thais to do this? Whatever it is, one thing is for sure: Thais do not take the whole business of eating lightly and its status within the realm of Thai culture is an extremely exalted one.

> 'The Thais take eating very seriously, so business
> people allow 2 to 3 hours for lunch. A formal business
> luncheon consists of several dishes, but most casual
> diners have a one-course rice, noodle, or curry dish.
> For two people, you'll be fine ordering two hot dishes
> and perhaps a cold salad (mostly of the "not spicy"
> variety). Most restaurants throughout the country
> offer lunch from noon to 2 pm; in fact, many close
> until 6 or 7 pm before reopening for dinner.' [7]

Although I now love Thai food and eat it pretty much every day, I have to be honest and say that, when I first came to Thailand all those years ago, I was not in the least bit interested in the local food. There were two main reasons for this: the first was that, if by some miraculous stroke of luck, I actually *was* able to work out what the dish consisted of, I still had the thorny problem of how to explain to the people in the restaurant what I wanted, and as anyone who has spent any amount of time in Thailand knows, trying to explain something in Thai, using a language that invariably has five different tones for the same word, is fraught with difficulty.

The second reason was that, because Thai food is so unique and quite unlike anything I had ever tasted before, I did not have an inkling of the sheer variety on offer with the result that I would incessantly order the same two or three dishes that I could name. Of course this soon became a bit boring when, every day, you are eating *Khao Pad Gai* (chicken fried rice), *Pat see you* (a mixture of stir fried noodles and green vegetables), or *Quit Deeow* (noodles in hot soup), and so this goes a long way to explaining my apathy towards Thai food in general.

Let me tell you a story as an example of the first reason e.g. being unable to explain in Thai what I wanted to order. Having being in Thailand only a few months, I was with a former farang girlfriend eating in a small outdoor restaurant in Pinklao. When we arrived and were seated, we could see from the other diners' tables, that the food looked really delicious, and so we were almost salivating at the prospect that some of the same food might wend its way to our table sooner rather than later. We were also extremely hungry.

When the waiter came, we attempted to order some food. I asked in my finest Thai accent, *'Rao ja ow preeow waan gai'* which I understood to mean, *'We would like to have the Sweet and Sour chicken'*. The waiter scratched his head, and then asked me to repeat what I had ordered. Again I said, *'Rao ja ow preeow waan gai'*. But again the waiter looked completely flummoxed and could not understand what I was saying. Then a nice gentleman sitting opposite intervened, but he too was as perplexed as the waiter. Not to be outwitted, the waiter then went and got some more waiters, as if he were the waiter Manuel, in a scene from Faulty Towers. However, like their colleague, these waiters merely scratched their heads in dismay. At his point, it seemed as if a convention was in town of collective head scratchers, much to our uneasiness and discomfort.

By now, both my girlfriend and I were starting to feel a bit embarrassed as some of the other diners were turning around to see what the mini-commotion was. Finally, the manager, or he may even have been the owner, turned up on the scene. He was a short, fat, bald Chinese looking man with a white string vest, a half smoked cigarette hanging out of the side of his mouth, dragon tattoos on the inside of each forearm and clearly visible heroin track marks to boot. Again I repeated what I had ordered, this time with a not insubstantial sense of trepidation not least because a few of the restaurant's diners, or at least so it seemed, were crowded around us, like a scene from a Monty Python sketch, hanging on every syllable of every word I said as if I were speaking a rare dialect version of a dead language. Finally, the string vest spoke. 'Ahh!' said he. 'I know! You want the sweet and sour chicken, is that right?' he enquired. 'Yes' we both said in unison, and everyone breathed a collective sigh of relief.

Chapter Notes:

[1] Churchill, Winston, in a speech as the British Home Secretary in 1910
http://achristian.wordpress.com/

[2] *Frog Commissary Notes, Steve's Notes, A Thai Sampler,*
http://www.frogcommissary.com/notes/thai.html

[3] *Thailand's Regional Cusines - Cooking Temple of Thai*

http://www.templeofthai.com/cooking/thai-cuisine.php

[4] Ibid, *Thailand's Regional Cusines*

[5] Ibid, *Thailand's Regional Cusines*

[6] *Thai Durian,* http://www.thaiworldview.com/durian.htm

[7] *Food & Drink, Thailand,*
http://www.frommers.com/destinations/thailand/0245020880.html

Ajarn.com

Blogs

2009-2011

The Thai Floods

When tomorrow never comes

31st October 2011

With the Asian Tsunami of 2004, the lack of a decent education, the rampant corruption, the near civil war last year between the Red and Yellow Shirts, and now the floods, you have to feel for the average Thai who seems as a resilient and flexible as on old leather bag. No sooner has one disaster come and gone, but another floats along like an abandoned Styrofoam tray. Now threats in the flood waters of crocodiles and snakes have been added to the mix. One wonders when, if ever, Thailand will settle down and Thais can enjoy a modicum of peace and tranquility. Or can they ever?

(above photo - Thai Businesswomen make their way through the floodwater as it advances into central Bangkok, on October 26, 2011

122

"Are you upset little friend? Have you been lying awake worrying? Well, don't worry...I'm here. The flood waters will recede, the famine will end, the sun will shine tomorrow, and I will always be here to take care of you. " (Charlie Brown to Snoopy)

Water, water everywhere...

Everyone knows how important water is to Thai life. You only have to look at the many rivers which coil around the land like a weaving snake; the monsoon season which covers Thailand's cities with a deluge of the liquid stuff; the myriad rice paddies; the water buffalos lazily grazing in fields; the variety of water-lilies and lotus blossoms in nearby ponds; the Tom Yum clear soup dishes, and a host of many other very Thai images that depend on water for their identities.

How sad now that the floods have been so harsh to the landscape and inundated the terrain smothering everything in its path. It's as if the Thai God of Water has put a curse on Thailand and opened its banks to usher in a post-deluvian world: a world where Thais have no choice but to wade waist deep in the thick browny liquid until sufficient supplications have been made at various temples and the god's anger subsides allowing the water to recede. For me though, better to put your faith in the gods, or Buddha, or an amulet than rely on your leaders, and this may partly explain the deeply held religious beliefs of your average Thai. After all, as the British like to joke - "The Romans, what have they ever done for us?" The same question could be asked by Thais - "Thai politicians, what have they ever done for us?"

Jam tomorrow...

Perhaps it's a bit unfair to say it, but it does seems to me that once again Thailand has been let down by its leaders. As usual the politicians have been busy figuring out ways to not say and do what should have been said and done at the start of the flooding, instead, preferring to protect Thailand's image abroad at the expense of the people who desperately needed help in terms of evacuation along with food and medical supplies. It's a familiar story in Thailand: tourism and the potential negative effects of a downturn were the main focus above helping the local population, just as the business sector was valued above the needs of poor Somchai and his wife in a paddy field in Loei.

123

With recent news that, as a last resort, the Thai army has been called in to help get the flooding under control, you have to wonder how and why a young, completely inexperienced female politician could possibly be in charge of a country of 70 million people? To say that Yingluck Shinawatra was as overwhelmed as the Mekong Delta is an understatement. The size of the monumental task before her would have tested the mettle of even the most seasoned politicians, so it beggars belief that she was left in charge of such a difficult situation, not just geographically, but one which has ramifications both politically and economically.

Those who remember Hurricane Katrina in America will see striking parallels in Thailand with the response to the disaster to the current flood. In fact, it seems as if every time there is an emergency or national disaster, the politicians and local leaders, instead of rising to the occasion like leaders should, see the opportunity in disaster and find ways to profit from it. As usual, what results is an "Alice Through the Looking Glass" scenario where things are promised but never actually turn up, hence the phrase "Jam tomorrow."

Disaster capitalism

This slow and/or inadequate response also happened when the H1N1 crisis came around as the government withheld information vital to people on the ground with the result that many people were in fear of just how much the disease had spread. The same scenario played out during the early stages of the 2004 Asian Tsunami where the potential for a disastrous impact on the local economy meant that many people didn't know how many had perished in the tsunami.

Perhaps someone can tell me why an event that happens every year, the rainy season, and has done since the beginning of time, has not been monitored to the extent that a clear, and well organized contingency plan exists for just such a disaster that we are all currently witnessing? Or am I being unreasonable here and expecting too much? I remember the words of a high ranking Thai water official who berated the government for repeatedly telling them, year after year, that they should make sure that the reservoirs in and around Bangkok and in other areas should always be emptied before the rainy season. Did the government, central or local, take a blind bit of notice? We all know the answer, unfortunately. No, this wouldn't have solved the flooding problem in of itself, but it would have mitigated some of its effects thereby lessening the impact on at least some of the country's denizens.

Of course a lack of leadership is prevalent not only in Thailand, but in other parts of the world today. Politicians like Angela Merkel, Nicholas Sarkozy, Christine Lagarde, and David Cameron, shuttle in and out of eleventh hour meetings in European capitals with the clear mandate to solve many of the world's economic problems that they should have prevented from happening. Yet, little ever seems to happen, and last week a high ranking European official was sent, not unlike Dickens' "Oliver Twist", cap in hand, and a begging bowl at the ready, to ask for investment from the powerhouse of Asia - China.

Those who want to find out more about this so-called Disaster Capitalism playing out in so many cities and countries around the world can read Naomi Klein's interesting book - "The Shock Doctrine". According to this doctrine, you need do the following: "Invest in "Disaster Capitalism. This new investment sector is the core of the emerging "new economy" that generates profits by feeding off other peoples' misery: Wars, terror attacks, natural catastrophes, poverty, trade sanctions, market crashes and all kinds of economic, financial and political disasters."

You could easily have added the banking crisis and the Credit Crunch to this list. I only hope that the negative effects of Disaster Capitalism do not happen in Thailand as they did in America where scores of schools were shut down forever and public services drastically cut back. Thai people deserve better: better leaders, better planning, and a better future.

Here's looking at you kid

How do those wonderful Thai folk really see us?

4th July 2011

Have you ever wondered what the Thais in your life think about you? I mean really think about you? Your girlfriend? Your Thai boss,? Your maid? The guy who washes your car? The motorcycle guy at the end of your soi? It may not be what you think!

I have often wondered what Thai people really think about us farangs? After all, Thais are really quite gentle souls who rarely say what they mean for fear of causing offence, and there is such an obvious chasm in terms of European and North American cultures when compared to Thai culture which, as we all know, has been a source of misunderstandings for many a decade. When you look at these differences closely, you soon realize that, in terms of the many races of people that visit Thailand's shores, with their own customs and social mores, non-Thais are like proverbial chalk and cheese, ying and yang, like night and day.

So, when you think about this fact, it may not come as too much of a surprise to find out that many Thais probably think of farangs as completely irreligious drunken fools with the shallowest of lives who rarely take care of their parents when they are old, who are impatient (jai rorn), and who often show their anger at the drop of a hat. But can we really blame them for making such assumptions about us? And are such assumptions really true?

Not a drop to drink

I chose this topic as my blog this time around primarily because of something I read on NottheNation.com this week. A Thai academic from Thammasat University was bemoaning the fact that farangs would be unable to cope during the alcohol dry spell because they seemingly cannot function without alcohol on a daily basis, and the upcoming election would mean that many, if not all, sources of alcohol would be closed for the days leading to the election. Personally I found her comments a bit insulting, as if the small few drunken farangs who go overboard is representative of ALL farangs in the kingdom or that without alcohol, they would turn into potential trouble makers. Here's what she said in an article called "Police Prepare for Election Day Expat Sobriety Riots Bangkok's - alcoholic farang population "unpredictable" as (quoted from NottheNation.com).

"For many of these men, 36 hours without a drink and the company of a rented Asian female represents something unacceptable, terrifying even," said Noppawan Rangkulan, sociology professor at Thammasat University. "Sobering up means becoming momentarily aware of their graying bodies and emotionally hollow lives. What we think of as an alcohol-free night represents an existential crisis for them."

Wow! That's a bit extreme init? Being unable to have a beer while on holiday represents "an existential crisis"? What was she on when she wrote that? I want some! I feel like telling her that an existential crisis is far more serious: what the likes of Sartre, Camus, and Beckett wrote about: Sisyphus pushing that dam heavy rock up that hill only to see it repeatedly roll down again, or Vladimir and Estragon waiting for a supposedly benevolent God to come and redeem them, but who never shows like an expectant guest-of-honour at a hi-so wedding; or young Meursault whose mother has died and he is so unperturbed by it, that he can't even remember when it happened or why it is important. No my dear, those are real existential crises!

Out of touch or right on the money?

But, aside from the obviously rebarbative comment from this academic, isn't there a lurching irony here? On the one hand, you have a country with an amazing (yes I chose that adjective deliberately!) tourist record - an average of about 14 million foreign visitors per year for several years now, who are feted and spoilt rotten with lovely women, cheap booze, sumptuous beaches and an array of pretty awesome food. Isn't it any wonder then that now and then these tourists go a bit overboard while they are on holiday? And anyway, isn't that what holidays are for: to overdo it and really let your hair down?

Yet, the more I think about these comments, I can't help wondering whether this Thai academic is right on the money, or completely out of touch with what farangs want or think, in the same way that, as I said above, there is a deep and abiding chasm between the general level of understanding between Thais and non Thais in general? Academics generally, in whatever country you care to mention, are perceived as other-worldly, "out to lunch", and as people who live in their heads or, as Sir Ken Robinson, the creativity expert said, "...are people who think their bodies are just vehicles for getting their heads to meetings"!

Moreover, the recent data at a news conference publicising the coming National Alcohol Free Day showed that heavy drinking has contributed to more than 100,000 divorces and separations in Thailand, while also causing 13,000 deaths and leaving more than a million injured. Smells of the kettle calling the pot black, doesn't it! I had to laugh too at the slogan dreamt up by the Thai Election Commission and, again, I didn't know whether to be offended or accept that this is the way Thais think of non Thai visitors to their country - "Stay home, stay wasted". "Due to the importance of this election, we are taking no chances with expatriate sobriety-related violence," said a stern National Police Chief Police General Wichean Potphosri. He justified the deployment of over 20,000 additional security officers nationwide as a necessary precaution against "deranged, sober foreigners." It seems now that farangs are more dangerous when they are sober which contradicts at least 50 years of social science data!

Anyway, given that the people who have the loudest voices and influence in Thailand see farangs in this way, the bigger question is whether your perception of your Thai friends and colleagues is the same as you think? Does Panit the motorcycle guy who drops you at the BTS every morning think you are a debauched alcoholic only three whiskeys away from a visit to AA? Does Nattavut, the guard at your condo building see you as a lech only after the cutest Thai females? Does Panida, your middle aged Thai boss see you arrive at work on a Monday morning and give you a look that says, "I know what you were up to last night you crazy farang!" And what about Koy, your Thai girlfriend? Ok...er...let's not go there! Here's looking at you kid!

From the Middle Way to the Middle East

Life as a teacher in the dunes

1st June 2011

When you've been teaching in Thailand for many years, there will eventually come a time when you want to venture out and try something different. This is especially true if you are getting "long in the tooth" and want some retirement money. Over the next few blogs, I'm going to focus on what it's like to live and work as a teacher in Saudi Arabia.

Hot, hotter, hottest

When I lived in Thailand, I used to joke with my students that there are three types of weather in the country: "hot, hotter, hottest!" This was always guaranteed to get a giggle and loosen up some of my charges. Of course, having come from a much colder European country like Ireland, and then brought up in the UK, I was always used to having four seasons, so quite naturally, I really missed the change between them when I travelled to Thailand.

I loved the crispness of a spring morning, the long, languid and lazy summer evenings, the panaroma of reds, yellows and browns of the dry leaves at Autumn, and the fun to be had at Christmas if you were lucky to have "a white one". This usually brought with it the potential for snow fights and a glass of the brown stuff while sitting round warming your hands in front of an open fire, the smell of a roast dinner only a room away.

The first thing to hit me when I arrived in Dharhan on the Eastern Saudi seaboard in February 2007 was the almost hairdryer like intensity of the heat. It's like sticking your head in an oven. As most people know, it's not a bit like the Thai heat which is very humid. Often, the heat in Thailand, because it's tropical, will have around 80% humidity, and this is the major cause of why you will sweat while walking out at lunchtime to get a sandwich from Deli France in Silom. In Saudi, you can walk around and almost never sweat although I wouldn't recommend it! From September to June it's bearable, even refreshing at times.

This is my favourite time of the year. You can stroll around in a t-shirt and there's often a cool balmy breeze to refresh you. However, when it gets to July, the hairdryer starts up again and even two minutes walking to a nearby shop will have you gasping when you returnindoors, and you'll be soon reaching for the "high" setting on the air con. There is also a real danger of heat stroke during these months as well, so it's really advisable to drink lots of water to keep yourself hydrated and to stay out of the sun wherever possible.

Compound life

As most people know, in Saudi Arabia, most foreign workers live on a compound. Ever since the 9/11 attacks, this has been mandatory for many embassies. The German embassy, for example, will not allow their citizens to live off compound and this is stipulated in every employment contract. This means that compounds are in high demand and, quite simply, there are not enough of them resulting in long waiting lists for expat families. This is especially true in Riyadh where there is a huge shortage of housing across the board. It also means that accommodation is very expensive as demand is high and the availability and indeed quality varies depending on where you go and who is managing it.

The staff on these compounds can be split into two groups. The managers and executives tend to be Indian while the general day to day ancillary workers can vary from Filipinos to Bangladeshis, Pakistanis and Sri Lankans. There's often a smidgen of Africans too such as Sudanese and Eritreans. There are very few Saudis among the workforce as they tend to be the owners of the compounds or shareholders.

An average compound will have at least one swimming pool, typically two or three (including smaller ones for the kids). Most will have a gymnasium, a squash court and a few tennis courts. The compound I first lived in Dharhan even had its own bowling alley, snooker and pool room, fitness centre, and 12 bars selling moonshine. This usually consists of non alcoholic lager or beer that has been imported and then yeast is added to make it reasonably palatable.

Personally, I don't much like this kind of moonshine as it tastes like someone has dipped a used sock in some putrid water, stirred it around, and then offered it to you. If you like a drop of the falling down water, you can buy some pretty decent homemade wine of the red, white, and rosé variety. You can also opt for something stronger what is known as "Sid". This is often up to 120% proof and will get you where you want to go in no time at all! Mixed with a drop of Coca Cola, tonic, or lemon it's a reasonable alternative to staying at home with a mug of coffee.

Down time

If I am to be brutally honest, there really aren't that many things to do at the weekend in Saudi Arabia. That said, you don't have to be down on your down time. Depending on where you are stationed, it really is what you make of it and, at the very least, there's always the compound and the usual shopping malls to investigate. If you live on the Eastern seaboard, you are only a hop, skip, and a jump away from Bahrain (which, in Arabic, means "two seas"). This place has been in the news recently for all the wrong reasons but is known among the Saudi expat community as the main pit stop for a bit of R&R when you want a beer or a lady or both, or just simply want to get away from Saudi for a few days. It's also full of Brits, with nice clean roads, organised traffic systems, friendly locals, and thousands of bars, malls, and restaurants to visit. It can be reached from Riyadh by plane in one hour or, if you are in Dharhan, you can cross an 8-mile stretch of road (read "bridge") called a causeway in less than one hour.

For the more sporty, outdoor person, Jeddah is a must see. It's on the Red Sea and has all the sports you could imagine from scuba diving, power gliding, jet ski racing, and a host of other outdoor activities. It is teeming with reasonably priced hotels and now the Saudi government is wising up to the potential revenue that can be had from promoting tourism and is actively promoting it as a tourist destination. If sport is not your cup of tea, you could always just lie on the beach and soak up the sun.

Lastly, where I currently am is Riyadh. It doesn't have that much going for it: crazy drivers on the roads, sand storms every few days, and blowtorch heat in the summer months. However, there are always a lot of embassy parties where you can mix and socialize and network if that's your thing. I recently went to the annual Janadriah Festival which celebrates Saudi culture (see picture above). There you can sample lots of Arabic food, see the various live music shows, and smell the famous Ood: a kind of Arabic incense which is simply amazing.

At Christmas and other festival times, there are often film festivals and various exhibitions to go to. I went to the South African Embassy last December to hear a choral recital of Handel's Messiah among other composers, some soothing Christmas carols, and it was terrific. Next week, as a member, I will go to the Irish Society's party at the Irish Embassy in the Diplomatic Quarter (known as the DQ). There will be a buffet style menu (finger food) from a highly regarded 5-star hotel, three drinks included (no draft, only canned variety) in the ticket price, and a band will be playing 80s hits. Can't wait

Thailand's new marriage laws

Marrying foreign men over 50 in Thailand – new laws

1st April 2011

"Separately, foreign marriages and whisky are bad; mixed, they are fatal. (Samuel Clemens aka Mark Twain - Letter to Olivia Clemens, 3 June 1895)

Three weeks ago, I happened to read in a newspaper that Cambodia had just passed a law banning foreign men over 50 from marrying Cambodian women. At the time, I thought it was just some kind of ridiculous joke. After all, just like Thailand, where would Cambodia be without the millions of foreign money that flows into its country on a daily basis? I mentioned this to some of my friends, many of whom have Asian wives, and they too scoffed at such a suggestion, but this is now law in Cambodia. Worse still in Cambodia, even if you are under 50, you need to now prove that you have US$2,580 per month coming into your bank or, again, you cannot marry one of the locals. Again, thinking it some kind of April Fool's joke, I read on Thaivisa.com this week that Thailand was considering something similar. Not to be outdone by its neighbours, Thailand is currently enacting legislation that will also do virtually the same thing. But why all the changes? What's all the fuss about?

Rationale for changes

In Cambodia, the reason behind the changes is that the government fears its country is becoming a major hub for child brides. A foreign ministry official recently explained that the government is making an effort to stamp out "fake marriages and human trafficking" and referred to cases of Cambodian women "used as slaves" abroad. But before we dismiss this completely out of hand, it's worth noting a few facts. On one hand this could be perceived as a smart move e.g. to deter pedophiles and unsavoury characters from marrying Cambodian women and then using them as prostitutes and/or as child brides elsewhere.

Yet on the other side, it also seems like a gross violation of people's basic human rights. What government has the right to say who you can or cannot marry? In most of the rest of the world, the mere suggestion that people from another country could be banned by their government from marrying outside their race would be an outrage, so how can two reasonably well-developed countries in Asia, Cambodia and Thailand, think this to be an appropriate response to a sempiternal problem e.g. of child trafficking and other similar pernicious crimes? Isn't it something of an overkill to simply deny a fundamental human right to choose your own spouse in order to wipe out another social problem? Have these politicians gone mad or is there a deeper issue here? Or maybe, just maybe, it's a further example of the quality of the leaders in these two countries and their level of reasoning and arguments that is showing itself to be yet again at worst, asinine, or at best, autocratic?

Strange political decisions

Thailand has had its fair share of strange political decisions over the years. Most recently, the RTG decided to ban the sale of alcohol in all areas where there are national parks. Ok, not a particularly odd law in of itself if you want to preserve the environment, until you realise that many of those national parks encompass holiday resorts like Koh Samet, Khao Yai and a host of others. Put it this way, if you were a tourist visiting Thailand, wouldn't you want to relax and have a beer or two while on holiday? Why too were all 7-11 stores banned from selling alcohol? What purpose could that possibly serve? Another example was the rule to remove Thai students with short skirts and pregnant students from state schools presumably in an effort to punish them by denying them an education or maybe to hide them away thus saving face?

My favourite was the suggestion by a former government minister, when bombs were going off in the restive south of the country, to pay many Thai Buddhist families to relocate in order to have them fight against the Muslims down there. Or how about the suggestion by another government minister, when there were marauding gangs of Thai motorcycle youths racing each other at night, to get gangs from other areas to race each other thus ensuring there would be brawls and one would wipe out the other. Er...yes...good one Somchai! Let's put that one on the statute book! Oh, and have a pay rise while you're at it.

What this all means for Thailand

You don't have to be a rocket scientist to see that a country that had 14.5 million visitors to its shores last year is clearly reliant and indeed dependent on the foreign dollar. To enact into law such legislation which refuses to allow a citizen to marry whom he or she chooses or even recognize a marriage overseas between a Thai and a foreigner, where the later is over 50, is complete lunacy. Xenophobia doesn't even begin to cover it. That said, the new law is in line with similar laws, as I said, in Cambodia and also Laos as part of the upcoming ASEAN integration in 2015. It is expected to pass Parliament with ease and should take effect on May 1st, 2011.

What effect will it have on the economy? Won't it mean that many will simply marry outside the country and be forced to either continue to remain married or get divorced in order to return? There are also rumours that there will be big changes in the rules governing inheritance from a foreigner which will again cause all kinds of problems not just for a wife of long standing, but also has repercussions for the offspring of such a union. What law will be next? Lollipops can't be sucked by Swedes visiting Thailand between July and August? Bathing suits can only be worn when accompanied by both parents and grandparents? Zebra crossings in Thailand can only be accessed if you step on the black lines?! (Oh, and by the way, Happy April Fools Day!)

Mr. and Mrs.

How many points would you and your significant other score?

4th March 2011

If you or your wife were asked ten questions about each other's likes, dislikes, favourite food, colour, smell, or what irritates you both etc., how well do you think you would score?

(Derek Batey (right) hands over to Alan Taylor, 2nd July 1975)

When I was a kid, I used to see a program on TV in the UK called Mr and Mrs. It was a kind of game show with a twist where a husband and wife would be separated in soundproof cubicles and asked a series of revealing questions about each other's better half. It was hosted by a schmaltzy English guy called Derek Batey, and the object was to see how well each spouse knew the other after many years of marriage. Of course that was in the 1970s where the divorce rate was much lower and where people stayed together in a marriage thus being able to say, with a degree of confidence, that they knew their wife or husband "inside and out"! I have occasionally wondered how myself or my wife would fare if we were asked to play - Mr and Mrs. I'd like to think we'd do well, but then you never really know do you, which begs the question - how well do you know your Thai spouse?

The kinds of married couples who appeared on the Mr and Mrs show were typically married for 30, 40, and in some cases, 50 years. Nowadays, not only are people separating faster than the straps of fake Gucci bags, but they are marrying, as I said in my previous blog, more and more from outside their own social groups, what are called exogamic marriages. This has added another dimension to the idea that a man and woman would necessarily know intimate details about each other. After all, how can you say you know and love someone if you don't really know the answers to revealing questions about them? Isn't communication everything in a relationship? And when your life partner comes from a completely different culture, with its own social mores and cultural expectations, doesn't that make it doubly difficult?

The problem

No marriage is perfect, and we all have our pet hates about what we perceive are the faults in our spouses. That well-known Thai-American songstress, Tata Young, wrote a song a few years ago entitled "Naughty, Sexy, Bitchy" presumably trying to capture the true Thai female, but she got into quite a lot of trouble for it from conservative as well as more moderate Thais. I have also often heard it said that Thai women are jealous, fiery, lazy, talkative, argumentative, acquisitive, and a host of other things that are as stereotypical as anything you might hear in a bar full of drunken men or a dentist's waiting room. But just how true is that?

Of course, while there exist cultural traits in every society, these kinds of generalisations are not helpful in finding out why so many exogamic marriages don't work out. Added to this is the fact that many of the exogamic marriages that fail only come to our attention because they have failed and are thus in the public domain in newspaper stories like the ones I talked about in my previous blog. I'm sure there must be many of these kinds of marriages that work too, but we never hear of them, or perhaps because the partners have gone off to the expat's home country never to be seen or heard of again.

With so little data on these marriages, it's hard to draw reliable conclusions. Do Thai spouses marry for love? For money? Or because they think the foreigner will treat them better? A study done in the north east by Dr. Rattana Boonmathaya from Mahidol University in 2006, revealed some interesting facts. The first is that the village chosen for the study was conspicuous for the fact that nearly one in three of the 330 women aged 20-59 resident there had chosen to marry a foreigner, but not just any foreigner. Amazingly 96 per cent had already married men from Switzerland. Why they had a penchant for the Swiss is anyone's guess. (Perhaps it was the chocolate!) Also remarkable is the fact that most of the foreign men marrying into the village were between 10-18 years older than their Thai brides, what I called <u>Morganatic marriages in my previous blog</u>. Again, as I said previously, the majority of both husbands and wives had already gone through previous marriages.

Another surprising finding by the academic was that the popularity for marrying foreign men appears to have become so strong among the women in the village that Dr. Rattana believed it had become a 'fashion', with the majority of girls of primary school age replying in the study that they wanted to marry a foreigner when asked what they wanted to be when they grew up. (Another Ajaran.com blogger focused on the meaning and relevance of this in a different blog). A prominent reason often proposed to explain why Thai women like to marry foreigners is to escape poverty, but even that cannot explain why the retired Thai tennis star Paradorn Srichaphan and his wife, former Miss Universe Natalie Glebova, recently informed the media that they are separating after three years of marriage. Aren't they superstars? Good looking and with lots of cash? So why wasn't that enough?

A personal perspective

Although I have only been married for close to four years, I have been with the same Thai lady for a decade, and like every couple, we have our ups and downs. Of course it goes without saying that I love my wife, but like all marriages, it's not perfect and just as I have strengths and weaknesses, so has my wife. My pet hate is when I'm trying to get things done and making plans. This involves projecting myself into the future, a characteristic I notice that most Thais do not seem to be particularly good at. I think it has something to do with Buddhism which grounds Thais into the here and now. It could also be because most Thais accept the tenets of reincarnation and believe if they don't get it right in this life, they'll have another chance in the next one.

When I typically ask my wife to do X mostly because it's (a) easier for her to do it (because it involves talking and/or writing to a Thai state employee regarding a bill etc.,) or (b) because I don't have time to deal with it because I am busy with other things, what usually happens is that my wife will invariably make a phone call or start out on a good footing. However, when that person is not available, or when she hits the first hurdle, she generally gets distracted and gives up. This is not to criticize her but to show that such behaviour, from what I've seen having lived in Thailand for well over a decade, is pretty common. It's a lasser faire approach to domestic issues. After all, why do today what you can put off till tomorrow, or "out of sight, out of mind" is king!

Another *bête noire* is when I ask my wife what she wants to do e.g. go to a particular restaurant, see a particular movie, or go to a particular resort for a holiday. She will invariably give me that old, clichéd response "up to you". What she really means is that you have to decide for yourself and her, but if it all goes pear-shaped, she won't necessarily blame you overtly, but she will be able to say she had no hand in choosing the activity that was selected thereby absolving her of any blame in the near future. (I touched on this in another blog about the <u>inability to take responsibility - Mai mee quam rapitchorp.)</u> Kirby, who commented on this in my previous blog has it just right:

"If your wife says 'up to you' on a particular decision-making matter, and you make the decision on this particular matter, then usually it is the wrong decision to her. She usually won't talk to you for 3-5 days after you have made the decision. I discovered this only during the first year of our marriage. I have now been married to the same woman for five years. She says it once in a blue moon now, but for me in one ear and out the other. I'll wait for her to make the decision when she does say 'up to you'".

You may or may not lay claim to know your spouse well. You may not even have been together very long, but if you're serious about each other, and have made, or are about to make, a long-term commitment, isn't it time you and your wife considered playing Mr. and Mrs?

How well do you know your Thai spouse?

Gruesome accounts of Thai wives who kill for money

31st January 2011

With recent newspaper reports showing a number of unsolved deaths of expats in Thailand, and with the finger of suspicion pointed squarely at their spouse, how concerned should you be that it could happen to you?

Those of you who read this blog on a regular basis will know that I mostly stick to issues related to education in the Thai context. However, in the next few blogs, I am going to look at the dynamics of relationships between Thai women and expats. The first blog focuses on the very notion of marriage between people from different backgrounds with a specific emphasis on how this works in Thailand. Subsequent blogs will focus on other aspects like the Thai female psyche, and elements like jealousy, trust and the legal ramifications of what happens when these kinds of marriages fail.

(above photo) Raymond Hinds' wife Fon and her lover Lek

Exogamy - *custom enjoining marriage outside one's own group. In some cases, the rules of exogamy may also specify the outside group into which an individual must marry. The severity of enforcement of exogamous restrictions varies greatly across cultures and may range from death to mild disapproval. (Encyclopedia Britanicca)*

How well do you know your Thai spouse? This question may seem quite absurd to some as marriage is a lifelong commitment and not one that is taken lightly. Yet for all the benefits of marrying outside one's own society: the opportunity to integrate into another culture, to learn another language, and to start a new life in a distant land, there are also many pitfalls as most expats reading this will have already experienced. In Thailand, although I confess I don't have the exact statistics, I think it's fair to say that most marriages are what are termed Morganatic marriages e.g. marriages between an older man and a younger woman where the man is considerably wealthier than the woman. Such men are often retirees, with one or even two western marriages behind them. While this may not be the norm, in practice, it is probably the most common type of exogamic marriage found in Thailand.

The British Embassy in Bangkok processes on average 70 marriages a week mainly between older Brits with young Thai wives. However, given the statistics for the global divorce rate show that two out of every three marriages fail, it is wise to consider how even more difficult it is to marry a foreigner, live in their community, and actually manage to make the marriage work. It should be remembered that when you relocate to a completely new country, communication between old friends and family is sometimes forgotten, adding to a feeling of isolation, and with it, a detachment from the social network and ties that stabilized and centred that person throughout their life. It should also be remembered that as the old saying goes, "many visitors old and new leave their homeland to travel to Thailand, but unfortunately they leave their brains at the airport".

The latest death

Many will have seen the recent newspaper reports of male expat spouses meeting their demise and the more than passing suspicion that it was at the hands of their spouse. The following is information gleaned about three cases from the following sources: Andrew Drummond's website - British pensioner clubbed to death in latest Thai wife killing. The Guardian newspaper - Thailand family and relationships The Times newspaper Thailand article

The latest death is that of 68-year old Raymond Hind from Cheshunt in the UK. He was a former garage owner who was clubbed and stabbed to death at his home in Hua Hin last May. What is interesting about this case is that two months earlier he had been attacked at his home and was so traumatized that he had decided to keep a shotgun in his bedroom. Just as distressing, he had been diagnosed with throat cancer and had clotted arteries and it was common knowledge that he was living on borrowed time anyway. Why then did someone kill him?

Attention immediately turned to his wife Bunnag known as 'Fon', 38, her brother, and her boyfriend, after Thai police failed to establish a legal case. After the murder, the Thai police held a press conference stating it was an open and shut case but, after mysteriously receiving bail, a deposition objecting to the bail was signed by thirty four Thai policemen. Fon's boyfriend, Thanakorn Bussa, admitted he had been commissioned by Fon to carry out the murder with her brother, Pomgrit. A knife had even been bought by Fon for the grizzly dispatching of her husband. Fon is reported to have told some policemen while in custody that £1.5 million (74 million baht) would be available in an obvious attempt at a bribe. Two close friends of Raymond Hind, also pensioners, have now put up £11,000 (530,000 baht) into a fund to begin a series of court actions on behalf of their murdered friend and his 30-yr-old daughter, Zoe.

Further gruesome cases

Two other cases deserve a mention. The first involved a Brit called Toby Charnaud, a former wealthy farmer from Chippenham, Wiltshire who was murdered in 2007 after he had divorced his Thai wife Pannada, 35. As the saying goes, "Hell hath no fury like a woman scorned" and she set about getting her hands on his estate through their son. The husband actually had a premonition of his own death and wrote a short story about it. He was beaten to death, and his body was barbecued then cut into pieces and scattered around Kaeng Krajan National Park near the Burmese border to be eaten by tigers and other wildlife. Pannada and two cousins were convicted of the murder and jailed for life in September 2008 after Charnaud's sister and parents in the UK hired a lawyer and private eye to investigate the case.

In 2008 Ian Beeston, a 69-yr-old retired engineer at the Ford plant in Dagenham, was beaten and stabbed to death by his wife's Thai lover in the north-eastern Thai province of Roi-et. According to an article in the UK's The Guardian Newspaper, the Thai police say he took seven hours to die after the attack at his house. Ian Beeston, like Charnaud, knew it was coming and had been waiting for his own death. He sat alone in his palatial home with a stun gun by his side to protect himself. He wrote a letter to his lawyers saying: "It is only a matter of time now. I am in real fear for my own life." His wife had already sold his land against his wishes. Thai lawyer Boonchoo Yensabai, an expert on these cases, who helped prosecute in the Toby Charnaud case warned: "In the worst of these cases if the wife has access she can, and will attempt to pay off the relevant authorities and foreigners will wonder may why the case is going nowhere."

What have you got to lose?

There are no doubt other cases where murder most foul has been committed but few of these cases ever reach court. In fact, you could be forgiven for thinking that Thailand is not the safest place to be if you are, aged, alone, and have money. This is especially true if you factor in the several suicides each year of expat men in places like Pattaya and Phuket, the motor vehicle accidents which often claim more lives or leave people dismembered, and the assaults or murder of expats and backpackers.

Only today I read that an unsolved case of a Canadian backpacker who was murdered in Pai three years ago has been solved and a Thai policeman has been jailed for 25 years. That's good news but may not be enough to allay the fears of those who see a crime rate among expats that is spiraling out of control. According to the Eighth United Nations Survey on Crime Trends and the Operations of Criminal Justice Systems, under the United Nations Office on Drugs and Crime, the Centre for International Crime Prevention, Thailand has a yearly average of 5,140 murders making it 8th of 49 countries surveyed.

Many do not understand that living in Thailand long term is quite different from having a holiday there, and there are many Thai women who believe expats have a limitless supply of money. Adding to this reality, many Thai men envy the fact that expats in general have more money than they do. Of course, not all Thai women and men are like this, and I'm sure the vast majority are decent, caring, law-abiding, Buddhist practicing citizens. That said, it would be prudent to think about what you've got to lose if you are already in a relationship with a Thai lady and contemplating marriage, or are a retiree just in search of a new start in Thailand. Besides your money, you could lose considerably more and so it might be wise to think about a pre-nup or finding a way to safeguard your children's inheritance by making a living will. It could just turn out to be one of the smartest things you ever did. Isn't it time you asked yourself that fundamental question - how well do you know your Thai spouse?

A longing to belong?

The Hotel California syndrome

2nd January 2011

Why do so many expats lose the plot after a while? Or put another way, with such a deep longing to fit in and belong, does living in Thailand make you a bit ting tong?

Going Native?

Having lived in Thailand for a few years now, a place I happily call "home", I have often wondered whether there is something about living in the kingdom that changes you in some way? I don't just mean the normal change that we all undergo: old age with hair loss, sagging skin, stained teeth, and a sense of creeping senility. I'm talking about psychological change that brings about a major shift in your thinking. I already touched on this in another blog entitled <u>Self-improvement in Thailand</u>

We all know that Thais quite often think we foreigners are a bit ting tong: a picnic short of a sandwich (if I can invert a well-known idiom), and who can blame them when they see bald, fat, western men flocking to their shores to grope admittedly willing Lolitas a quarter of their age? Who wander round in various stages of stupor as well as undress, complaining about the heat, the food, or the traffic? At the last count, 15.8 million tourists visited Thailand and, let's be honest, they're not all here for the food, the beaches, and the scenery.

Given that Thailand is such an attractive place to live, it's not surprisingly that there are many who come here and decide to stay. Some settle here and, by and large, blend into their surroundings and assimilate with relative effortlessness; others outstay their welcome and are summarily deported; and yet there appears to be another group that persists in staying here (or frequently leaving only to return) while not really seeming to (a) fit in or (b) enjoy their lives here.

Such people whine continually about how difficult it all is. It is this latter group that, for me, is worthy of a few comments in this blog for they appear to get more eccentric in relative proportion to the time actually spent in the host culture. They are facing what I like to call the Hotel California syndrome or, as the words of the song succinctly express: "you can check out any time, but you can never leave".

You say tomato, I say...

Of course, it could just be that the people who tend to come to Thailand and stay here, tend also to have a degree of eccentricity or ting tong-ness in them already, so this can't be ruled out. Or it could just be the low cost booze, the access to cheap beachfront hotels and friendly women. I ask this question because I have come across so many people here who are not what you would call regular or normal in any sense of the word who've tried to check out but find they can't.

Yes, I know there is no such thing as normal in the real world as we are all unique, all different and complex human beings, but there is usually a pattern that people follow - a certain identifying mark like a fingerprint that helps you recognize people with similar backgrounds who have made particular choices. It should also be remembered that Thailand has long been well known for people to come and hide out from the long arm of the law. I include rapists, murderers, child molesters and a host of others running away from something, possibly even something within themselves which of course is an impossibility, and something of a paradox.

Indeed, it's fair to say that, other than the criminal fraternity, what we might loosely call the Gary Glitters of this world, the fruitcake teachers like Mark Karr who admitted erroneously to killing the child star JonBenet Ramsay, the vast majority of people who come and visit here, and who end up as expats, are what might loosely be called educated travellers - well-educated people with degrees and a penchant for adventure. And having travelled extensively in Africa, the Far East and Europe, I have met a lot of these people who might be called eccentric at best, or downright quirky.

I remember a few years ago sitting in the bush in Ghana while having a conversation with a thirty-something American lady and sampling the local plant life. She opined that all travelers are to some extent eccentric. She reasoned that the very fact they were willing and indeed wanted to leave the safety of their motherland meant that they were not your normal 9-5, square peg in a square hole kind of people. Their sense of wanderlust was a symptom of a deeper malaise - a sense of being different and not being able to fit in and indeed function properly in their homeland. This, she explained, was the reason why they had to travel - in order to find a place where they could fit in.

If you want an illustration of what I mean about the oddballs that visit Thailand's shores, you have only to look on other pages of this board to learn of someone who continually bleats on, in a misogynistic way, about Thai and Filipino females referring to them as whores, who sits around composing his rants posing as blogs in his y-fronts while watching Fox News, and who lacks any sense of judgment in posting a picture of his students without permission in a wholly unhealthy and questionable context. Such people have been here too long and seem wholly bereft of any understanding of what it means to live in harmony with their hosts and their surroundings. They misrepresent their students, upset their colleagues, and argue endlessly with their peers. They are an eyesore who stand out like a proverbial sore thumb; a gargoyle on the side of a building which has no other function than to scare others and spew out rainwater.

Lights, camera, action

Of course, when such people find themselves unhappy in their own country, it's inevitable that they'll seek greener pastures elsewhere, so in that sense, when they move on, one culture's loss is another culture's gain (or loss, depending on your perspective). This theme of belonging (or not) has been well covered in the movies and literature. Who can forget Marlon Brando's portrayal of Kurz in Scorcese's Apocalypse Now, who runs away from the US army, secretes himself away in the jungle and becomes a kind of mad tribal chief who encourages his flock to hack off limbs and behave in a psychotic way? Or Richard Harris in A Man Called Horse who plays a white man captured by Native Americans who eventually assimilates into their culture? Or John Blackthorne from James Clavell's Shogun; an English sailor shipwrecked in old Japan who decides to learn the language to fit into the unfamiliar society, and eventually decides that it's preferable to the society he came from.

Whichever character you look at, it inevitably doesn't end well for them, and for many in Thailand, this is also the case. When the alternative is to return to a place like England that seems to be permanently cold or raining, with high taxes, crap public services, or America, where the health system favours only those with money and cripples those financially who become sick, what choice does there seem to be?

A Hobson's Choice or no choice seems to be the only rational answer! It goes without saying that it's a human instinct to search for a place to call home, a place to belong. The Thais place great emphasis on the home and family and know that, which is probably why they are so forgiving. Indeed, you have to give credit to the Thais that they are, by and large, prepared to endure us westerners and our idiosyncrasies and treat us with respect even when it is not deserved. For that, we owe them a debt of gratitude. At the end of the day, it should be remembered that, like the song says, "we are all just prisoners here of our own device" so it's up to us to make the best of the situation we find ourselves in and not cause too much of a problem for our gentle hosts. We at least owe them that much.

The students are revolting

Would Thais ever follow the actions of their fellow students abroad?

7th December 2010

With British students and others across the world up in arms about the cuts to education budgets, brought about mostly because of the Credit Crunch, Thomas Tuohy offers some reasons why Thai students rarely revolt in the education sector in Thailand even though the quality of their education is and has always been so poor.

Those of you of a similar age and cultural background will remember the Lux soap advertisement on TV from many years ago which involved a quasi-Russian family flying in a private jet. They were all in luxury baths onboard the plane soaping and lathering themselves in the lap of luxury. One member of the family looks down on the peasants below and remarks that they are "revolting" thereby introducing a pun on the word e.g. that they were both dirty (being peasants) and rioting because of some perceived injustice.

Up in arms

Over the course of the last two or three weeks, we have seen on the news the stories of British students revolting at what they perceive as unjust: the proposals to reduce UK degrees from 3 to 2 years, the shortfall of government funding to the tune of 30% over the current government's term in office, the removal of all government funding for school sports, the knowledge that the quality of British education is suffering with large intakes of foreign, mostly cash-laden, Chinese students with the concomitant drop in standards, and that the costs of UK degrees are set to spiral out of control to the tune of £36,000 for a typical three-year degree course. (I wrote a blog about it here if you are interested)

Unsurprisingly, in times reminiscent of the 1970s, where student unrest was rife, there have been demonstrations, sit ins, and unhappy students prepared to voice their concerns at this problem caused by the introduction of "austerity measures" (don't you just love that phrase!) especially given that tens of thousands of places have also been removed for students to attend colleges or universities across Europe. Last week in France, tens of thousands of students and teachers across the country joined together to protest a $10.2 billion cut in education and research funds. The day before the general strike, over one million workers and students clashed with riot police in Paris after a demonstration over university reforms.

As one commentator wrote - "Universities across France have been barricaded and picketed for almost two months in a standoff over these higher education reforms. The satirical weekly Le Canard Enchaîné recently reported that Sarkozy wanted student protests calmed by May, fearing echoes of the student-led protests of May 1968." In Barcelona too, seven people were arrested and 80 injured in clashes between police and university students. The clashes occurred during two city-centre protests in the northeastern Spanish city after police forced students out of a university office they had occupied since November. In Italy, students threw shoes and other objects at the police in front of the ministry of the economy, copying what had happened in France, and the Italian education minister stated that, as a result of the cuts, 18,000 teachers will not find work this year while 10,000 will be employed at universities on an ad hoc basis.

Could this ever happen in Thailand?

For all the general mayhem that has been flashed across our TV screens, you not only can't help but sympathise with those students, but you also feel a sneaking regard for them sticking up for their rights. In fact, this highlights a major cultural difference between the young of Europe and the young of say, Asia. European, and to a large extent North American, children are taught to be independent and critical of their environment from a very early age. They are taught to stand up for themselves and be counted and to fight for what they believe in. In contrast, Asian children are taught much less febrile qualities like subservience, allegiance to a higher power: parents, their superiors (teachers, elders, the king), and to make an effort to belong to a group.

Of course, while I don't wish in any way to denigrate these qualities, as they are admirable and belie the gentleness that is uniquely Thai, in general, they do not lend themselves to unrest or to be willing or able to do anything about the paucity of a quality education. This has been a constant problem for Thailand and, as we saw with the April riots this year between the supporters of the Red Shirts and the pro-government Yellow Shirts, the divisions and fissures are still there, but they are played over a much wider spectrum, and are more akin to good old-fashioned class riots rather than having an angry protest about something as important as an education. The fact remains though that, as I have commented on in other blogs, even though over 30% of the total Thai budget is spent on education in Thailand, a lot of it ends up as graft and therefore in other people's pockets not on books, access points for internet, school facilities, higher salaries for teachers, and so on.

What history teaches us

Of course, these days, there may be a good reason why the youth of Thailand doesn't revolt given the clampdowns in 1973 and 1992 where student protests resulted in many deaths of protesting students. In May and June of 1973, students and workers rallied in the streets to demand a more democratic constitution and genuine parliamentary elections. When October came, more violence continued with protests about the detention of eleven students arrested for handing out nothing more explosive than anti-government pamphlets. Later, the demonstrations grew in size as students became more vocal and demanded an end to the military dictatorship. On October 13, more than 250,000 people rallied in Bangkok at the Democracy Monument, resulting in the largest demonstration of its kind in Thai history. The next day, Thai troops opened fire on the demonstrators killing seventy-five, and then occupied the campus of Thammasat University.

However, while this is deplorable, as Napoleon said, sometimes "History is a collection of lies agreed by others" so what didn't necessarily work in the past, could end up working in the future. It is a marvel to me that so many hardworking Thai students have had themselves and their country held back by such a relatively small group of poo yai people who have been creaming off the country's resources for more years than most care to remember. In addition, the inability to share out the country's wealth has created a huge divide between the rich and the poor and held back generations of genuinely talented people. You have to wonder what it would be like if Thais were actually more like their continental or American cousins? Would they ever again dare to occupy an institution as hallowed as Thammasat or Chula? Would they ever dare to question the mechanisms of power that ensures that the money always stays within the hands of the same poo yai families irrespective of which party is in power? And even if they did, what difference if any would it make?

Nowadays, more and more people are becoming pro-active in taking up the rights they should be enjoying, but are not, and they are beginning to protest in non-violent ways which is a particularly refreshing thing to see. One event happening on December 7th which was suggested by the ex-Manchester United striker, Eric Cantona, is for thousands of people all over France to withdraw their savings from French banks simultaneously. The idea is to cause a run on the banks to return the power to the people. While the cause seems noble enough, we'll just have to wait and see if it actually happens. However, it is clear that we have entered an era where the ordinary man and woman in the street is much less willing these days to accept the status quo and that can only be a good thing for everyone. For me, the only thing that is truly revolting is the inequality that exists in today's supposedly developed societies.

Professional development

Adding a few strings to your bow

29th October 2010

It is always wise to spruce up your CV by adding a certificate or two; teaching a course you never taught before such as TOEIC or IELTS, attending or presenting at a language workshop; or simply going to a language teachers' convention like ThaiTESOL.

Keeping tabs on the market

Nowadays, given the state of the world's finances where good jobs are hard to come by, nobody needs to be told that, whichever job you do, it's always a smart thing to keep abreast of the latest developments within your field. This means if you're a language teacher, you need to make sure your CV is up to date and that you can show you've made an effort to develop yourself as a teacher. We all know that living and working in Thailand has a lot of pluses, but one thing is absolutely certain - little or no emphasis let alone money will ever be placed or spent on you as a teacher in a typical Thai establishment.

If there is any money available in Thai schools and universities, it has been my experience that it will almost exclusively be spent on local Thai teachers, and personally I don't really have any problem with that. The fact is Thai people will often see your value as someone who is already an expert and who can provide something in a classroom. Continual professional development (CPD), while it may be very fashionable in Europe and North America these days, has yet to catch on take a hold in SE Asia. In fact CPD if it exists at all in Thailand, as I said is something that your hosts will probably expect you to take care of yourself. What specific things therefore can you do then to make sure you stay ahead of the game and make your CV and experience stand out where others wilt in the shade of a potential recruiter's office?

Take a course

The first thing to do is to look through the list of schools you have worked at and assess your overall attractiveness to another school prior to submitting an application for a new job. In other words, try to think of yourself from the point of view of a training manager or headmaster. Evaluate your experience. What specifically can you offer that school that makes you stand out? So many educational establishments these days are looking for that person who can offer something unique: someone who has a teaching certificate that also has e.g. some component related to kids like art work skills or musical ability.

If you can play an instrument, put it on your CV. If you wrote a paper on classroom management, include that, too. If you ever did voluntary work in Africa, Chile, or Romania, again make sure you put that down. If you're nifty hand with Excel or Outlook, make it known. If you have an opportunity to visit a language teachers' convention such as ThaiTESOL, put your name down. They normally host a major event in Bangkok every January (and alternate every other year in Chiang Mai) and have done so for the last 30 years. At the very least, you will have an opportunity to meet like-minded people and possibly network and make some new friends along the way. If you can't find anything to shout from the rooftops about, you need to sign up for a course.

It can be a frustrating experience to go for interviews, not get the job and not really know the reason why. My wife recently applied to the British School in Riyadh. She sat there in the waiting room and, in talking to others soon realized that she wasn't as qualified for the job as she had imagined even though she has an education degree and bags of classroom experience over many years. Even though the job was only for a Teaching Assistant, one lady was an accomplished piano player and music teacher; another was a native speaker of 30 years experience in a nursery school; unsurprisingly, my wife wasn't successful in her application. I have now been able to persuade her to do a postgraduate certificate in childhood education online in the UK. While it may not yield her a better job right away, it will keep her busy while I'm at work, her gain a new certificate and, who knows, it could open a door or two in the future.

CPD in the classroom

According to Wikipedia - "CPD can be defined as the conscious updating of professional knowledge and the improvement of professional competence throughout a person's working life. It is a commitment to being professional, keeping up to date and continuously seeking to improve. It is the key to optimizing a person's career opportunities, both today and for the future." However, most people tend to associate this with graduates and/or working professionals seeking to improve themselves by acquiring news skills usually while they are already in the workplace although this is not always entirely true.

Last year, when I taught a Business and Management English summer course at the University of Birmingham, I was there for only 10 weeks. During that time, I was invited to 12 separate CPD workshops on topics ranging from how to use e-Boardwork in the classroom, a Listening and Pronunciation workshop, using TurningPoint, classroom teaching software, and many others. However, while it was amazing to have the opportunity to be a part of so many free workshops, the CPD offered by this hallowed institution didn't stop there.

In the classroom, as a teacher, I was also required to get my students involved in a form of CPD themselves. When they were asked to prepare their group as well as individual presentations, they were also required to reflect on all the problems, obstacles, agreements, disagreements that became evident throughout the process of creating the presentation. This included what ideas they decided to include in their data collection and which ones they decided to discard including their rationale for doing so. All of these elements were required to be logged and presented in a document which was included as part of their assessment and also became part of their overall mark. This process encouraged them to focus on the very processes that helped produce a hopefully successful presentation and to help them identify areas that caused them problems with a view to being better able to avoid the same problems in the future. Again, this was also a form of CPD albeit a reflective one in its practice.

If you're a teacher in Thailand who feels in a bit of a rut and looking to secure a better job somewhere else, now may be the time to dust off your CV and think about some ways you can make yourself attractive to a future employer, a time to add a few strings to your bow. I promise you - you won't regret it.

Taking responsibility - Mai mee quam rapitchorp!

We are more than just robots with marker pens.

3rd September 2010

How many teachers have really thought about their responsibility as a teacher in a classroom and the effect their teaching can have on future generations of people - lawyers, doctors, teachers?

If I've learned anything on this planet after 46 years it's this: nobody seems to take responsibility for their actions any more. I know- I sound like an old man, like one of those old fisherman who bemoans the world he now lives in and wishes it were like it was when he was a child. "It weren't like that in my day you know!"But I can remember being told that that was part of being a good citizen e.g. that you took responsibility when you stuffed up, when you made a pig's ear of something, whether intentional or not, and stood up and said "mea culpa".

Most people do not really want freedom, because freedom involves responsibility, and most people are frightened of responsibility

sigmund freud

In those days, there was a much more keenly felt sense of justice and fair play and a clear moral compass for guidance where even politicians routinely resigned when there was only a whiff of a scandal. Nowadays, you can't even get convicted criminal politicians to serve their time in prison, so if our leaders won't show us the way, what hope is there for the rest of the populace?

OK, I admit that Thailand is not exactly well-known for having its citizens go out of their way to shoulder the burden of blame when the proverbial brown stuff hits the fan, but I do think us westerners could show them a thing or two about how to admit when you're wrong and observe how this can be a catalyst for change when it happens, instead of pretending the problem never existed in the first place and not ever discussing it.

When it all goes wrong

How many teachers are willing to admit that they have never really sat down and thought about the impact their teaching has had on their charges and what responsibility, if any, they have to those students' futures? How what they teach, and the ways they teach it, have a direct impact on those same students? And what happens when it all ends up in disaster? When something that the student learned in the classroom causes a problem in later life, or just as significant, what they didn't learn and perhaps should have?

The idea that we as teachers can just breeze in and out of students' lives and not have any lasting impact is surely quite mistaken. As teachers, we are often directly responsible for shaping the minds of our students, their attitudes, encouraging them in ways that don't always have anything directly to do with a particular curriculum, the ways teachers teach students not just how to express themselves in new and interesting ways, but also in how to behave in certain situations and, most importantly, to know the difference between right and wrong.

We are all so busy these days that we scarcely have time for ourselves any more so it's not surprising when we hear of more vocational college students fighting in rival gangs and where an innocent nine-year old boy is shot in the face and neck and killed on his way to school. These students seem bereft of any moral guidelines and behave like thugs with complete impunity. What too of the responsibilities of the teachers of those boys to prevent them from attacking each other with guns and knives? Or even the responsibilities of their parents? There seems to be an ethical vacuum in these people's lives and goes partly some way to explaining their completely callous acts this week.

Who's responsible?

I got to thinking about this while researching an article about a German doctor Dr. Ubani with poor English language skills who accidentally administered an overdose of a painkiller to a patient, David Gray, 70, while working for a health trust in the UK last year. There was so much finger-pointing but nobody wanted to accept responsibility, not the doctor, not the Primary Care Trust (PCT) that employed the doctor, not the organization that controls foreign doctors working in the UK.

I mention this also because it was the first time I had come across a possible link between the results of poor language classroom study and its possible consequences. Here was a highly respected overseas doctor with twenty two years experience who had not been able to communicate well with a patient to establish his problems and made a critical mistake. Does it matter that the doctor was of Nigerian descent, a native speaking German forced to speak English in a country where he'd only had three hours sleep upon arrival, and where he was also having to drive his car on the opposite side of the road for the first time ever in an unfamiliar environment? Probably, but the net result is the same - someone is now dead.

Mea culpa?

I started to wonder if I as a teacher have ever been so poor in the classroom over a sustained period of time that I could have unleashed unto the world a few Dr. Ubanis of my own who were plying their trade with all the skill and aplomb of a deep sea diver in full metal diving bell suit! I've had a few dud students over the years as has every teacher. I define "dud" as a student not unlike an unspent cartridge - you know there's something there but you can't get it to ignite, can't quite get a spark going in the eyes of that student; can't seem to get them into a good learning pattern or help them develop some aspect of themselves either educationally or any other way. We've all experienced such students in our classrooms, so it isn't hard to imagine.

When I was a teacher in Saudia Arabia for the first time, I was teaching Saudi Air Force cadets Aviation English, and I can tell you that I had quite a few duds there. To give you a simple image, "the lights were on the runway, but there was no planes taxiing because the pilot was out to lunch". These cadets were being groomed for the workshops where the planes were serviced. I'm talking about million pound aircraft like the Harrier jump jet, the Hawk, the F-15 and others. I have often wondered how many of them mistakenly used wrong tools to install or repair old or new equipment? Perhaps there's aircraft in service now with ill-fitting bolts, cranky and loose wheel bearings, palm oil being used for lubrication instead of aviation oil?

Could I be responsible for that in some way? Abdullah and Achmed are working on a 10 million US $ jet. Abdullah: "Is it a 9-mm capstan screw?" Achmed: "No, it's a 12-mm staple." Abdullah: "Never mind, stick it in. The plane will fly. Inchallah!"
I've taught doctors and business managers too, and been responsible for teaching many other skilled and unskilled people. If I haven't done a good job in the classroom, could I have endangered the lives of some doctor's future patients or, like the butterfly and Tornado example used in Chaos Theory (Does the Flap of a Butterfly's Wings in Brazil Set off a Tornado

in Texas), could I be a link in the chain of events that brings about an end that is not would I would have liked or intended in any way?

I guess we can only thank god that we are not often asked to take responsibility for our actions because, if we ever became aware that in some small token-like way, we were part of a series of processes that ended in calamity, then it would become increasingly difficult to ever step into a classroom again. That said, we are more than just robots with marker pens, and it never does any harm to remember that what we bring to the classroom can and maybe does leave a lasting impression on all our students.

Skirting around the problem

Why focus on issues that have nothing to do with problems in education?

30th July 2010

Why do some in Thailand choose to focus on an issue that has little or nothing to do with Thailand's problems in education?

I read in The Nation this week about something that somehow appears with the regularity of similar yet irrelevant stories I find in the UK during the summer months when parliament is closed. Journalists there call it "the silly season" because, in the absence of any real news, journalists, social commentators, and media personalities resort to stories that were formerly presented in editorial meetings, but were rejected because they were probably a little frivolous, a tad lightweight, and also because, at the time, there were probably other more pressing stories to report.

Getting a dressing down

The current story doing the rounds here is thus an old chestnut because it has little or no bearing on the quality of education in Thailand and, if you've been here a while, you will again have noticed the usual pre-occupation with the length of female students' skirts' as if somehow that has anything to do with their performance in their respective schools.

This was the headline:

The Office of the Private Education Commission (OPEC) has warned private vocational schools they will be shut down for a week if they have students who are inappropriately dressed.

You could have, tongue in cheek, remodeled this to say they have "warned the privates to watch their privates", but irreverence aside, why oh why are we routinely subjected to this almost petty insistence that female students dress in a way that suits middle aged males whose idea of fashion and grasp of modernity involves having a latte once a month in Starbucks? In an age when people are supposed to have democratic rights and freedoms, which of course also means freedom of the body, why are they routinely ignored in favour of a conservative policy that seeks to deny them any clothing rights at all? And why, if these colleges truly are private, are they having these external judgments passed over them?

Just as important, why are these banal topics regularly raised when so many critical and more pressing problems are evident in the Thai education system? What about the huge shortfall of qualified teachers? The embarrassingly low salary offered to them? The results of tests for teachers which showed the vast majority in the sciences failed tests in their own subjects? The tests conducted on headmasters and school executives where 95% failed them? The fact that many vocational college students regularly fight each other with knives and guns and people die? Why pregnant teens are expelled from school as a form of punishment? Why recently a young Bangkok University student was stabbed to death by other students in a public place? Why are these problems not being given priority instead of trying to punish young teen girls for doing what all normal healthy girls in all countries do anyway?

The reasoning

The apparent logic behind these rules can be found in what the current Office of the Private Education Commission (OPEC) director Charnwit Thapsuwan said, which was that his office had received public complaints about students in Bangkok wearing inappropriate uniforms - especially skirts that were "too short". Mai oh mai! Young girls in short skirts! In Bangkok! Whatever next! You have to marvel at a country that produces places like Nana Plaza and Patpong, where prostitution and gambling are illegal but which still flourish, and where corruption is so ingrained in the social fabric that a poll found that most Thais don't actually mind corruption as long as the people committing it - politicians, policemen, poo yai leaders of industry etc. - actually do something for the country as well!

Charnwit Thapsuwan also said that "...students who overly expose their flesh could become the victims of crime...", and he also encouraged parents to watch what clothes their children were wearing. This is a bit like asking Jack and the Beanstalk to look after a trillion ants below his feet because the modern parent of today has little or no time to be acting like a "clothes policeman/woman", checking on a daily basis whether their children are appropriately dressed or not. And anyway, as soon as they leave the house, out comes the mini skirt and the tight blouse so it is impossible to police such a policy.

Moreover, when a thriving sex industry is allowed to flourish, it is hardly surprising that young women are overly sexualized at a young age because, in failing to clamp down on such illegal activities like prostitution, the government is sending a message, albeit subliminally, that dressing in a sexual manner is ok.

Double standards

These double standards are one of the main reasons why Thailand lags behind other S E Asian nations in its development as a mature nation. On the one hand, you have conservative leaders who regularly make comments which are more of a distraction than offering any real help in solving the country's problems. On the other, you have a populace which is largely young and tech savvy, and which is in tune with the modern world through peer websites like Facebook, YouTube, and MySpace among many others.

This juxtaposition is really a contradiction in terms. It's a bit like trying to chase a train that has already left the station or close a suitcase that already has too many items packed into it. Both activities are largely futile and what would make more sense would be to develop a policy that recognises that young people are living in the modern world and are constantly bombarded with images from the internet, billboard advertising, shopping malls, I-phones etc., etc., and where they see overt forms of sexual behaviour from a very early age.

The punishment should fit the crime

The article in The Nation went on to say the following: "OPEC had notified private vocational colleges to get tough on such students. If there continued to be complaints about any college's students, the institution would be asked to explain and could end up being punished by having all classes suspended for one week, as per regulations, Charnwit said."

164

Again, this is meant as a deterrent, but do they really think that shutting down the offending institution would (a) actually solve the problem or make it go away? Or (b) that denying students their education is the best way to deal with something that they perceive as impolite behaviour in their conservative interpretation of what constitutes a decent society? Surely, keeping them in the school or college would serve a much greater purpose but only if an attempt were made to actually offer classes to try to understand the situation from the point of view of the students themselves? This would be preferable to a knee-jerk reaction of sending home all students from a college irrespective of whether it was actually any of them who were wearing inappropriate uniforms? For me, this is yet another example of people in power simply skirting around a problem instead of facing it head on and dealing with the underlying reasons why young women want to dress in this way.

Two heads are better than one (sometimes)

some reasons why the education sector in Thailand is so poor

6th July 2010

The problem

It is a well established fact that without a sound education, a solid grounding in what used to be called the Three Rs (Reading, Writing and Arithmetic), it is very difficult to get on in life. All the more reason why the people who administer education in schools, whether they be the practitioners themselves, the teachers, or those who manage budgets and generally organize the day-to-day schedules, are often given a somewhat elevated status in the eyes of the denizens of a given community. Such people are prized because they have attained a high level of education and, as such, are entrusted with passing on that knowledge to others in their community. It is here that we are reminded of that old Chinese proverb - "Two heads are better than one". Or are they?

Some of you may have seen the well-written and interesting article by Sirikul Bunnag in The Bangkok Post recently. It was entitled - "School heads lack English, ICT skills - Poor survey showing surprises authorities". What was interesting about this article is that it highlighted a major problem in Thailand or, more specifically, a problem that exists with the administrators who run the majority of Thailand's schools - from the headmasters and executives, to the board of directors themselves.

A survey was carried out by Srinakharinwirot University earlier this year to test the abilities of about 40,000 school directors and deputy directors under the jurisdiction of the Office of the Basic Education Commission (OBEC), a government department connected to the Thai Ministry of Education. No doubt this is part of Thailand's increasing efforts to become a "knowledge economy" in line with its Second Educational Reforms.

The Results

The results may shock you though as it was discovered that two major areas where one would expect the executives and headmasters to be not only adept, but highly skilled - English and IT - were found to be seriously lacking. "Many school executives are poor at English and technology," commission deputy secretary-general Saneh Khaoto said...although Mr

Saneh declined to reveal how poor many school executives were at English and ICT."

One can only assume that it must have been pretty bad if they won't reveal the exact numbers, but at the risk of sounding churlish, what surprised me most was the response to this dilemma. Instead of admitting that these no-doubt highly-skilled people needed both IT and English language skills, the bulk of the money set aside to correct this anomaly was earmarked for other activities like "morality" training among other equally irrelevant areas. OBEC has apparently spent 678 million baht on the tests alone which is a staggering amount when compared to the amount which was allocated to actually fixing the problem.

As the writer of the original article says - "Another 500 million baht will be spent on promoting morality among teachers and 60 million baht on e-training." Forgive me, but two obvious points spring to mind here - what has morality got to do with making senior manager and executives better at English or IT? Moreover, why, when the problem has been clearly identified as an English language and IT problem, is more than eight times the amount being spent on morality training? Indeed, what has morality got to do with management at all?

For me, this neatly sums up some of the problems inherent in the Thai education system. On the one hand the government spends "...678 million baht on the tests alone" in an effort to identify problems, and then, when those problem have been highlighted, they are seemingly ignored in favour of something that has little or nothing to do with the original problem.

Indeed, other aspects of this survey do not ring true either. "The office did not expect this, because most school executives have master's degrees." The underlying assumption here is that just being in possession of a master's degree automatically confers ability in (a) the English language, and (b) IT.

This is of course a complete fallacy and something of a non sequitur as we all know that many senior positions here are often got through connections, for example through one's family e.g. nepotism, and/or through long term associations like friendships formed in schools or colleges e.g. cronyism, so to have ignored this fact is to have been taken something of an ostrich in the sand approach to problem solving. It is hardly surprising then that the true problem was completely overlooked and a lot of money seemingly wasted on what I can only classify as excessive bureaucracy.

What others say

Judging by some of the many comments left by readers on the bottom of the page where the article appears, it's pretty clear to me that others feel the same way. "I think they should fire them all if they fail the test. How can you teach if you can't pass? Disgrace." While I think this is a bit harsh, I do think it is not unreasonable to argue that those who are in high positions in academia should, at the every least, have the requisite skills to pass their own tests using whatever criteria that may entail.

Another more cynical reader wrote "Why are people surprised that English and ICT are so poorly taught in Thailand? It's what the powers that be want. Too many people with a good knowledge of these two subjects would be dangerous because they would be in a position to read and listen to information from sources other than government approved ones." Whilst I am not someone who would ordinarily listen to such an obvious conspiracy theory, it does seem strange that for all Thailand's wealth and its abundance of human capital, it seems incapable of developing that resource to its full potential?

We don't have to look too far into Thai political history to see that there is a large and developing chasm between those who feel disenfranchised (the Red shirts), who feel totally let down by a system run by an elite in Bangkok (the so-called "amata"). If we have learnt anything from recent conflicts in Thailand, it is this: that there are many who feel that they are being let down by their education or lack of it or, as Einstein neatly put it - "The only thing that interferes with my learning is my education". Perhaps this is a case where two Heads really aren't better than one?

Breaking news or broken news?

Will the true story of the mayhem ever be told?

1st June 2010

What happened to the reporting of the recent troubles in Thailand and the responsibility of foreign news journalists to report objectively?

The problem

Those of you who read this blog will know that I normally steer well clear of anything remotely political, but I couldn't pass this particular topic by without commenting on it as it affects everyone who lives here. Whether you are a long-term expat like me, or a Thai wanting to see your country represented in the international media in an honest and unbiased way, you will no doubt be dismayed as I have been by the recent coverage of the riots in Bangkok over the last few weeks.

Those of us who witnessed this destruction, whether on our TV screens, Facebook, YouTube, or in the flesh, will no doubt have been truly shocked at the scale of the general mayhem and the lack of intervention by either the police or the army. We saw thuggery and lawlessness on a grand scale paid for by a demagogue, now in exile, and fomented by so-called leaders whose own vested interests seemed to be the only thing important to them.

However, for me what was most shocking was the reporting of the carnage by foreign media outlets from experienced journalists who seemed to have popped off a plane and hunkered down with the Red shirts as if that was the only side of the story that needed to be told. I am of course referring to two particular outlets - CNN and the BBC - who seemed to offer daily reports on first hand accounts from the Red shirt leaders yet never thought it necessary to also get first hand accounts from the other side, too - the Royal Thai Government.

This news was not the "breaking news" kind that we see on our TV screens: news that makes us sit up and pay attention because we know that something awful has happened; genuine and truthful news that engenders something deep within us, which rises up and unnerves us, something atavistic that demands our attention. No, this was broken news because it presented a side of the story that was wholly at odds with what the vast majority of Bangkokians knew to be true - that the Red protestors were not merely innocent little victims practicing a kind of Satyagraha (Ghandi's concept of non-violent struggle), but that they too were offering a violent reaction to what they perceived as a class war against their amata masters in Bangkok.

To have not understood this was to completely miss the point leading inevitably to shameful reporting. It reminds me of "Yellow journalism" at its worst: a kind of journalism or storytelling that reverts to the lowest common denominator. In this case, that dynamic was what is commonly used when scandals break out, what the sociologist John Thompson calls "scandal syndrome". We had Watergate, the general lying that characterized the Nixon presidency, DianaGate, the events surrounding various scandals connected to Lady Diana, and many more.

In Bangkok we might have called it the "David and Goliath" syndrome where the aforementioned media outlets decided to present their coverage as a kind of "Big guy, Little guy" scenario, but where the little guys, the Red shirts, held the moral high ground and thus were automatically right. From there it inevitably followed that they, the media, as the so-called "guardians of democracy", needed to show them in the best possible light

170

irrespective of whether they were in fact lobbing grenades at BTS stations and killing innocent civilians on their way home from work, or setting fire to businesses and shops that ordinary people, fellow Thais, had worked hard to build up.

Other commentators

I am not the only commentator to have noticed this complete abnegation of responsibility as journalists to remain objective and to report only the facts in as transparent and truthful a way as possible. Andrew Biggs in his column in The Bangkok Post had this to say: "But CNN has really upset me over the last two weeks and it's not only an isolated news report. I have watched helplessly as Dan-somebody and the aptly-named Sara Snide - or is it Snider? - reporting breathlessly from the red shirt camp. Their new friends are freedom fighters battling the evil Thai government in the name of democracy. Bangkok is burning! Will good old-fashioned country folk triumph over the evil military? Will democracy survive? There is a difference. Dan and the Snide woman have been so slanted in their reporting that all they have forgotten is to tie a red scarf around their heads."

In an open letter to CNN International, which was also posted on Facebook, Alice Witheker Zeze Na Pombejra, a Thai citizen also had some scathing words for the two journalists: "Mr. Rivers and Ms. Snider's choice of sensational vocabulary and terminology in every newscast or news report, and choice of images to broadcast, has resulted in law-abiding soldiers and the heavily-pressured Thai government being painted in a negative, harsh, and oppressive light, whereas the genuinely violent and law-breaking arm of the anti-government protesters - who are directly responsible for overt acts of aggression not only against armed soldiers but also against helpless, unarmed civilians and law-abiding apolitical residents of this once blooming metropolis (and whose actions under American law would by now be classified as terrorist activities) - are portrayed as righteous freedom fighters deserving of worldwide sympathy and support. This has misled the various international Human Rights watchdogs to believe the Thai government is sending trigger-happy soldiers out to ruthlessly murder unarmed civilians without just cause."

The Role of the Media

Of course it's a well-known cliché that you should "never pick a fight with an organization that buys ink by the barrel", but someone needs to stand up and say when the media has transgressed, and during the Bangkok protests, it's clear that at least two media outlets got it seriously wrong. Sad though it was that a number of foreign journalists paid with their lives for the opportunity to report on the mayhem, this does not let them off the hook. The golden rule of journalism is that you should not become the news, but the history of journalism is littered with instances where journalists got it badly wrong.

The most famous case was that of South African photojournalist Kevin Carter. In 1994, Kevin Carter won the Pulitzer prize for his disturbing photograph of a Sudanese child being stalked by a vulture (above). That same year, Kevin Carter committed suicide because he later realized that, in the ruthless pursuit of getting the perfect picture, he had lost his humanity by not rescuing the young girl who later died.

What this tells us is that journalists are human and can mistakes like the rest of us. Though by and large they do a good job, they are not immune to criticism either and more often than not these days, with the exception of the BBC, are merely mouthpieces for large corporations whose paymasters demand nothing less than the observance of their own personal views and convictions writ large for all to see.

Will the true story of the mayhem in Bangkok ever be told? Frankly, I doubt it but, with the social websites like Facebook and YouTube, a new form of democracy is being ushered in: one that allows us all to witness first hand the atrocities that are being perpetrated in the name of democracy. In future, the news that is fed to us by large corporations may still be "broken", but now we have the tools to see for ourselves what really happened. We can see through another lens and can thus frame our own opinion.

Native vs non-native speaking teachers

Who would you employ?

2nd May 2010

Who to employ?

This is an age old debate, and one that never seems to go away. If you ask one person the question above, you get one answer, ask another, and a different answer will be given. The fact is nobody can really say what the better deal is from the perspective of a school owner. But what if we change the perspective slightly and ask the same question from the perspective of a student? What would a typical student say in response to the same question? No doubt you'd get a similar cross-section of opinion with some opting for the native speaker, and others for the non-native one.

But, at the risk of turning this into an over-simplification, or sweeping generalization, shouldn't we all be in agreement that it's nigh on

173

impossible to categorise people in such a general way? I mean, there are as many good non-native teachers as there are bad ones and, in the same way, there as many good native speaking teachers as there are bad ones, too, so quite often when we make such generalizations, we forget that there is good and bad in equal measure whoever you employ.

One story

Having worked alongside both native and non-native speaking teachers over the years in places like Thailand, Saudia Arabia, Ghana, and the UK, I have to say that I have always been impressed a lot more with the latter. Perhaps it's because they have to work harder and are generally paid a lower salary, so they may feel a sense of inadequacy because they don't have attributes that certainly most Thai language school owners prize - blue eyes, blonde hair, and/or a degree from an English speaking country like say, Australia, the USA, or the UK.

I once tried to get a colleague, who I had worked with at the University of Birmingham, a job in a reputable institution in Saudia Arabia. This gentleman has three masters degrees, two bachelor degrees, and has worked as a teacher in a variety of roles in places as diverse as Iran, Argentina, the UK, Brazil, Pakistan, Oman, The Czech Republic, S. Korea, and Canada. He had also presented at conferences in countries as varied as Hungary, Argentina, and Azerbaijan and has published more than 131 academic papers to date. When the interview came around, which was a telephone one, all went well as his spoken English is impeccable. Of course the question eventually arose as to whether he was a native speaker or not. As he was born in Pakistan and held a Pakistani passport, it mattered not a jot that he was more qualified and experienced than 90% of chalkies and had spent many years in native speaking countries living and working. His application was sent "upstairs" for consideration by the powers-that-be in the institution concerned, and a refusal to consider him for the position was returned a week or so later.

What this tells you about some institutions is that they are blind to the incredible talent out there and will refuse someone with obvious skills and experience simply because they don't fit a particular racial profile sad and true though this is. It didn't even matter that this teacher was also a Muslim and prepared to teach in one of the strictest Wahhabist societies in the world. In other institutions, this would have counted as a plus, but not here.

Another story

Conversely, my wife works in a well-known international pre-school or kindergarden in the centre of Bangkok. Here they will employ non-native speakers more often than not instead of experienced and qualified locals or native speakers, but only if they are white-skinned, with light coloured eyes and hair. I remember one time my wife told me that they had employed a blonde, blue-eyed, Swedish girl who had no experience, no qualifications, certainly no teaching qualifications and, I believe was degree-challenged as well. Although she was employed as a teacher, and had classroom duties as well, she was paid 40,000 baht a month basically to look pretty when the moms and dads came in the morning and afternoons to bring and drop off their kids. This was basically pandering to the lowest common denominator and had little to do with pedagogy or education whatsoever.

Pleasing the punters

The saddest part of these kinds of stories is that the main reason why native speaking teachers are preferred over their non-native speaking cousins has little to do with things like the ability to use RP (Received pronunciation) and be able to talk like the man on the BBC six O' clock news or talk like Bill Gates e.g. with an American accent. If that were the case, then there would be some reasonably sound arguments that could be put forward to say why such teachers are preferred. On the contrary, more often than not, native speakers are preferred because little Somchai won't be left alone with an Indian, a Pakistani or a Phillipino because they are often perceived as dirty or stupid or incapable of giving little Somchai the kind of education he needs or deserves. Similarly, such students are often handed over to a good looking young female with dubious qualifications simply because the parents, who know little about what constitutes a good teacher, value such things above true pedagogical awareness and experience.

Of course this is a very shortsighted perspective and is a waste of very valuable skills and resources but, let's be honest, is it ever likely to change while parents have a say in the school they choose for little Johnny or Navaporn?

Self improvement in Thailand

The *sabaii sabaii* problem

28th March 2010

If you haven't already noticed it, you will sooner or later. It creeps up on you like a shadow at the end of the day. What am I talking about? I'm talking about the sabaii sabaii dynamic in Thailand which doesn't encourage you to do anything meaningful with your life; a dynamic that says it's better to "go with the flow", "bend with the breeze', and observe the status quo - all aspects that are uniquely Thai. Of course, for a good while, this way of life will not only satisfy you, but will make you think about the horrible rainy days you left behind in London, the oppressive heat and drought of Brisbane, the cold damp skies of Berlin, or depending on where you're from, the negative things you left behind. You'll be captivated by the friendliness and charm of the Thais, the easy no fuss aspect of their natures, the ease with which you can get away to a beach, a club, a golf course or whatever is your poison all at a minute's notice.

Perhaps it's me, but at some point several years ago, I realised that the *sabaii sabaii* thing wasn't working for me any more, and I was stuck in something of a rut, both personally and professionally. I was in a relationship with an English girl that didn't appear to be going anywhere, and I was in a job that required me to go through the usual hoops of teaching, going on the occasional team-building exercise or open day, or taking part in typical extracurricular or pastoral activities, but I wasn't really satisfied and didn't really feel that I was improving myself in any way. In short, I was bored and wanted something that would lift me out of the doldrums.

Making changes

I managed to get out of the 3-and-half year relationship, but still I felt that something was missing. I was, like so many long-term teachers and general expats that stay here for a while, who try to learn the local lingo and succeed, to some degree, in turning their back on the culture that they were brought up in.

The problem with doing this in Thailand though, as most expats will already know, is that it's very easy to vegetate in Thailand, as Thai people, lovely and friendly as most of them are, don't really go in much for self reflection or professional development. The most common practice for the average Thai is to find a little niche somewhere and pretty much stay there till they can't anymore. There is very little emphasis in Thai culture to push yourself as the "mai pen rai" dynamic pretty much rules the waves, and the culture is steeped in phrases that promote harmony, relaxation, and living a stress-free existence.

There's nothing inherently wrong with the sabaii sabaii lifestyle, but after a while it starts to grind you down, and the minutes become hours, the days turn into weeks, the weeks into months and, before long, you realise that a whole chunk of your life has disappeared before your eyes and you can only look back and wonder where it went. Like John Lennon famously said - "Life is what happens when you're making other plans."

Unsurprisingly, as I said, I got caught up in this dynamic myself and, after a while, yearned for something that would stimulate the old brain cells, the grey matter which seemed to be decaying rapidly. I tended to find myself seeking out likeminded people who wanted to talk about intellectual topics like the three you're supposed to avoid in Thailand, what I have called the "Trinity of Untouchable" - the monarchy, the government, and Buddhism. I wanted also to be able to talk about literature, philosophy, good books, food, politics, new discoveries in science, anything that had some depth to it and was therefore interesting enough to make me think. I wanted feel alive again, and discussing topics that forced me to evaluate and be critical about the world I lived in again, seemed very attractive.

Re-educating yourself

Great though it was to connect with people on an intellectual level, I still felt that I was stagnating intellectually, and so I decided to bite the bullet and look around for a study program that would get me thinking again about topics that have some depth to them. Consequently, I enrolled on an MA Writing program via distance learning at an Aussie uni called Swinburne University of Technology. There I met a lot of people who were interested in talking about similarly highbrow topics, and my intellectual as well as spiritual awakening began.

From there I gravitated to some other postgraduate programs in Australia like one in Project Management, Leadership and Communication, and Entrepreneurship, and finally to a PhD Writing program that is almost complete. The fact is that something needs to be done when you have reached this stage although it doesn't need to be as radical as my experience. Even just taking up a hobby like sailing or collecting beer mats is a good thing, (although the Aussie woman arrested in a bar in Phuket for trying to take a beer mat home as a souvenir, may disagree with me!), anything that gets you out of your slumber, your comfort zone, and helps you find a hinterland.

I chose education because that is something that I am involved in professionally, and it is quite appropriate given that Thailand is going through its Second Educational Reforms which means, as a country, it's trying to promote a system of lifelong learning for all its citizens.

So, my advice to all those expats out there who've been in the kingdom for a few years and are already in (or nearing) that phase (which is like a kind of cultural jetlag) is to begin by taking one small step at a time. When you come home for example, don't do what 95% of expat men do in Thailand and head for the fridge for a cold beer. Pick up your mobile and call a friend for a game of tennis or a similar sport. Instead of turning on the TV, read a book or go out for a walk in the early evening. Find something that is a change to your routine, something that challenges you in some way, and I promise you, you'll feel much better for it.

Government initiated projects in Thailand

What is being done to help people in times of economic hardship?

3rd March 2010

Past and present efforts by the Royal Thai Government (RTG) to initiate projects to help the unemployed in Thailand.

Having been living in Thailand on and off for more than 13 years, I have often wondered about the amount of government initiated projects that are, or have been, offered and paid for by the RTG? In most countries, especially during periods of economic decline, projects are proposed and financed by central government in an attempt to reduce the number of unemployed, and to see that job opportunities are made available to those who want or need them.

For example, when I was a youngster growing up in London, there were schemes like the Young Trainee Scheme (YTS) where young unemployed school leavers and the general unemployed could get technical skills to enable them to have a better chance of finding paid employment. Such skills included basic welding, mechanics, bricklaying, indeed the full range of vocational as well as manual labour type jobs. I have been surprised to find that few if any of these kinds of programs appear to exist in Thailand, or if they do, they are not all that well publicized.

English for Interviews

One program, however, that I remember well and which was initiated by the first Thaksin government was a program conducted by the Go International program via the Continuing Education Centre of Chulalongkorn University in Bangkok. It was called "English for Interviews' and, if my memory serves me well, was a program that lasted for about six months. At one point I even remember that Thaksin's own son Pangthongtae attended, although I was spared the responsibility of having to teach him myself. The main focus of the program was to get unemployed graduates from Chulalongkorn University (and maybe Thammasat University) back to work.

To be honest, given that the courses consisted mainly of Business English, I am not entirely sure how much use they were to Thai students who would, in the vast majority of cases, have been interviewed by Thai managers and administrators in Thai. However, by all accounts the program was considered a huge success, and many Thai students graduated from the program with some degree of advanced knowledge in things like how to answer interview questions well in English, how to prepare for an interview, what to say in answer to tricky questions, what questions to ask, how to prepare CVs, and covering letters, and so on.

From a teacher's point of view, the work was great as you were guaranteed six months work, at 30 contact hours per week and paid at 800 baht an hour which was a decent sum in those days! If you did well on those courses, you were also offered more work in the corporate section of Go International which I believe is still alive and kicking to this day.

New government initiative

I mention this program now because I have recently heard that another perhaps similar program is about to be announced in the coming weeks as our most esteemed website owner, Phil, recently announced the following information on his home page: "Chatting to one of our regular ajarn contributors this week, he had it on good authority that there is to be a new government initiative that could create literally thousands of jobs for foreign English teachers in Thailand. We'll try and bring you more news on that as and when we get it, but it would certainly be a major boost for foreign teachers in Thailand. Things haven't been easy over the past couple of years. This would be very welcome news indeed."

Given how quiet the EFL sector is at the moment, we can only hope that the contract is extensive, the hours long, the pay great, and the possibility of more permanent work emerges on the horizon. Watch this space as they say!

The Thai TESOL conference 2010

ELT in the next decade: sharing, caring, daring

1st February 2010

The Thai TESOL Conference 2010
"ELT in the Next Decade: Sharing, Caring, Daring"
(held at the Twin Towers Hotel, Bangkok)

This weekend, I accepted an invitation to look in on the Thai TESOL Conference in Bangkok. Let me share my observations.

Thailand TESOL requests the pleasure of your company on the occasion of its 30th anniversary celebration. We will be celebrating this auspicious occasion with a buffet reception.

Room : Kasatsuk 2
Twin Towers Hotel
January 29, 2010
6.00 - 9.00 pm

Although I've been a teacher for a good many years, I am not one who usually has much time to attend conferences, whether academic or any other kind. The fact is, I have always shied away from these kinds of gatherings as I had it in my mind that they were populated with lots of avuncular, professorial types in hunting jackets, smoking pipes, and tilted their heads to the right, like Sir Ken Robinson, the creativity expert says in his amazing TED video "...who live in their heads and see their bodies as just a vehicle for getting themselves to meetings!" (link at the bottom of the page)

However, I have to say that I was pleasantly surprised at the event as a whole. There were lots of interesting people there, an ambient atmosphere, chatty interludes, interesting presentations, shared life as well as classroom experiences traded, and overall, comfortable surroundings in which to forget about the outside world for a few hours.

Although I was there principally to arrange an interview for the English Language Gazette newspaper with the president of Thai TESOL, the engaging Assoc. Prof. Ubon Sanpatchayapong, I was kindly offered an opportunity to see for myself what was planned for the two-day event from 29-30 January, 2010.

(The president of Thai TESOL, Assoc. Prof. Ubon Sanpatchayapong addresses the delegates.)

The Welcome Speech

The conference began with a welcome speech by the esteemed lady above. She talked about the present aspects of the conference, how the theme of the conference - "ELT in the Next Decade: Sharing, Caring, Daring" was to be understood by us all in this industry and that with delegates from over 30 different countries represented, how we can pool our resources in sharing our knowledge. In terms of caring, she talked about the support from many institutions for the ELT sector in Thailand which helps us care for our students. At times too, we should be daring ourselves to take risks in this ever-changing multicultural world, as well as seeing these challenges as a stepping stone towards ensuring the students to go the extra mile even if that means making a mistake and daring to be wrong.

This opening speech was followed with the keynote speech by Khunying Kasama Varavarn Na Ayudhaya, who gave an inspired talk about the three most influential teachers or educators who affected her as a small child, what she termed as opening the "three black boxes". She mentioned a famous book series called the "Little Lulu" series which I personally have never come across, but would like to, and she reminded all the delegates how important a good primer of a book can be as a good introduction to the English language for small children, although as she said, this particular one is now sadly out of print.

This made me reflect on how important teachers are to our own development and further about the list that might make up my "three black boxes"? Who were the teachers that influenced me? I once had a teacher called Mr. Tomashewski, a Polish woodwork teacher in London, who was very strict and would always make us stand behind a line that was drawn (with military precision) exactly one metre from his desk. I am not sure what I learned from him, for I cannot say with any conviction that he was either inspirational or likeable. However, he did teach me to begin something and then finish it like the wooden newspaper rack I made for my mother and which I abandoned at least two times before he took me to one side and showed me how to complete it. This made me realise that even the teachers we don't feel much of a connection with have something to teach us.

Another, perhaps who might have made it onto my list, was a headmaster who took me under his wing when I was at boarding school, and he always had an ear for me when things were bad and I got into trouble - a regular occurrence. The fact is, my school days were far from inspiring as I had about as much interest in education as an elephant does for sleeping in a roomful of mice. Funny of course, nowadays, as I am a teacher and heavily involved with learning in one shape or another. The phrase "Poacher turned gamekeeper" springs to mind.

(Edward Geerson and Assoc. Prof. Suchada Nimmannit host the Graduate Student Research Forum.)

The first plenary speech

After the keynote speech, we were treated to the first of the day's three plenary speeches by Prof. Chris Davison, an Australian academic who is heavily involved with designing and developing the educational curricula in Singapore, Hong Kong, and Brunei, and who appears to be a proper dyed-in-the-wool English language academic. She talked about Assessment For Learning (AFL) and how as teachers, we should all strive for assessments that directly help the students and are integral parts of the educational and pedagogical dynamics, not simply an instrument that is used exclusively for grading and ranking students. In other words, she suggested that we use this as an educational tool as well as deciding that little Johnny is X level and tiny Navaporn is Y level simply based on a written or spoken test.

I thought her story about using this assessment methodology in Singapore was quite funny as she quoted the eminent educational theorist, Michael Fullan, who famously said that "It takes at least 7 years for a new educational development to be successful anywhere" and in Singapore, Chris Davis was told "we can do it tomorrow as our students are very diligent!" Ah!! If only it were that simple!!

Other worthy mentions...

Some other presentations of note were the following: Gail O'Connell gave a great talk about how to use pronunciation strategies that will help the students understand why particular words are stressed in a particular way. She had a sentence on the screen which was something like the following:

"I want you to see that it is this one, ok?"

She showed how you can get the students themselves to come up with ways to add emphasis which might focus on the original person speaking (I), the person receiving the information (you), the main verb (want), the second verb (see), the object (it) and so on. I found this interesting as we rarely if ever get the students to think about sentence stress themselves before we offer ways to separate and thus delimit possible meanings in a sentence ourselves.

Kristjan Bondesson also gave a good presentation about "Incorporating Local Insights into Materials Evaluation", and one that had delegates' feet and fingers gently tapping in other seminars or workshops was that given by the indomitable David Quartermain. You can probably work out why given the title - "From Classical to Hip Hop - How to Really Use Music in the EFL Classroom".

All in all, a fascinating look into the world of Thai TESOL and not one crinkly, head-tilted-to-the-right, octogenarian professor to be seen anywhere!!

Link: http://video.google.com/videoplay?docid=-4964296663335083307#

Tom Tuohy is a teacher and writer. His interview with the president of Thai TESOL, Ubon Sanpatchayapong, will be published in the EL Gazette in their April 2010 edition to coincide with the IATEFL Conference & Exhibition in Harrogate, Yorkshire, the UK.

The domino effect

A look back at the EFL world in Thailand throughout 2009.

11th January 2010

As we reach the end of 2009, a lot of things have been happening in the EFL industry in Thailand. EFL companies are either falling like dominoes or radically altering their business models.

"If you go down into the woods today...you're in for a big surprise." Ok, maybe not "the woods". Perhaps that should be changed to something more urban as in "the city of Bangkok" because if you do chance to take such a stroll, you'll see that there have been some very surprising things happening of late, particularly in the world of EFL. You'll find for example that there have been so many companies slashing their advertising budgets, altering their business models, changing business premises, taking on new partners, or folding altogether. Given this pattern, it would seem that many EFL related companies in Thailand are all falling like proverbial dominoes!!

The year started well enough in January with the usual Thailand TESOL conference, so the year began with a relatively normal beginning. It should be said that this coming year, Thailand TESOL is 30 years old in 2010. To celebrate, the organizers will be holding the 30th International Conference from January 29-30, 2010. They have decided that the theme of this conference is "ELT in the Next Decade: Sharing, Caring, and Daring". Do please give them your support.

Domino Number One

As the year progressed, we had a scandal or two though which began with the debacle that was English+ and the subsequent lawsuit that became fodder for journalists at the Bangkok Post and The Nation. It seems Mr. Manoch, the entrepreneurial owner, was unable to control his staff who regularly turned up for classes drunk or in a pretty sorry state ("three sheets to the wind" if I may use a sailing metaphor!) and many of his franchisees, who paid a considerable amount of money to use the brand name, and his teachers, have now filed a lawsuit. Watch this space as they say.

Another stalwart of the Thai EFL business, that has had a torrid time since the Credit Crunch and the global recession, is Elite which has changed offices from the Silom Road base (above the Korean Air shop) it has occupied for longer than anyone can remember. If this were America, we would say that the owners are "downsizing", but let's be honest, nobody gives up long established and apparently successful business premises, and continues trading, unless something is radically wrong, right? Or is it a case that in this recessionary period they are in fact "upsizing" like those offers you get at MacDonald's for a bigger Coke? Um, not sure. I'll let you be the judge. When I emailed the powers-that-be, I was directed to Vannop Tanrudee, and I was told that all was well and that they had just taken on some new full time teachers. "We just opened [sic] new school branch at Sathorn road mid of this year, and just recently recruited new full-time teachers for our new young learner programmes. Absolutely no truth from [sic] your rumours." So there you have it - straight from a particular animal's mouth. (I have refrained from using the full idiom in the possibility that I may later be sued for defamation...)

The Rumour Mill

But perhaps the biggest of the dominoes, which may not have actually fallen, but has radically altered the way the company does business in The

Land of Smiles, is EF (Thailand). I spoke to Jean Scurti, the Senior Operations Manager, who assured me that yes, there were some changes in their business.

"EF Thailand, the division which is run by EF Education has absolutely no intention of closing. We have business partners in Thailand, franchise school [sic] in Bangkok, which are closing but we are not closing EF in Thailand. In terms of advertising, I do not oversee marketing, and it is not in my realm to comment on rumors about advertising spending." For me, this is a strange comment to make from someone who signs off as the "Senior Operations Manager for Thailand" but who doesn't seem to know anything about the marketing or advertising budget. The words "pass" and "buck" spring to mind!

When pressed for further information she responded with the following, "This year we have reviewed a number of our business partnerships in Thailand and taken the decision to discontinue some of them. Our head office remains in Bangkok, providing educational services to young people, students, adults and members of the business community." Again, watch this space as they say.

The Thai Culture course

The mandatory Thai Culture course has always been in the news since it started in 2006, but there have been a lot of people this year voicing their concerns albeit behind the safety of an avatar on ajarn.forum.net and elsewhere. In 2008, there was also a petition that was posted by one well-known teachers' agency (who shall remain anonymous), the Thai owners of whom have been quite vocal about what they perceive as treating farangs in a despicable way. It seems to me that they are unhappy only because they themselves are getting less and less of an opportunity to exploit the farang teachers who get paid peanuts and who have to often travel upcountry in order to serve their paymasters in Bangkok.

I had to laugh though when I read this for it neatly sums up just how far a Thai school owner will go in order to be critical of their superiors at The Teachers' Council of Thailand, the ministry that oversees the test which determines whether a teacher will be awarded a teaching license or not.

"WE feel that this is another way of extorting money from foreigners who wish to teach in Thailand and highly unnecessary in time and cost. WE urgently request that you send a written objection to this email address to be taken personally to the Ministry of Education to protest this course. WE ALL NEED YOUR SUPPORT!!!" Three more words spring to mind - "Pot" "kettle" and "black".

Like any petition that, on rare occasions, gets started in the Land of Smiles, it came to nothing as one would expect given the price for making criticism public - blacklisting, failure to have a visa or work permit renewed, or even worse, deportation. Like the German officer used to say, during interrogation in the old movies, "Resistance is futile!" Nuff said. If the rumours are to be believed, the Thai Culture course will soon be scrapped anyway, or allowed to fade quietly away as if it never existed, which is the uniquely Thai way of discontinuing deeply unpopular practices thus saving a degree of face.

One wonders what else is in store for the world of EFL in Thailand this coming year? Whatever it is, I hope it's good! Have a great 2010!

The maturing of the Thai EFL industry

Something tells me there's a bright future ahead

1st December 2009

I began this column for ajarn.com some six months ago with a look at the way that writing is taught in Thailand, and I bemoaned the fact that there is a dearth of creative writing programs which allow Thai students to better develop their critical and creative thinking processes. I focused on the exceptional creative writing program offered at Lanna International School in Chiang Mai as an example of what can be achieved e.g. because its students won a major international award for their creative writing.

This for me was one of the signs that something good is happening in terms of education here, especially though not exclusively within the language teaching and learning environment; a sign that there is a clear and blossoming element which is an indication of a maturing of the language teaching sector as a whole. What we are seeing more and more of these days, are the different ways in which Thai and international students can access new language, and through a much wider set of mediums e.g. satellite links to classrooms, more blended learning, new and more modern teaching methods, external validation of courses, and international recognition of Thailand as a great place to study for international students.

Another example has been the commitment by The Royal Thai Government (RTG) to raising the standards of teaching here by providing money to provide a better standard of education for all Thai students. This has been part of the Second Educational Reforms (the First being in 1999) and the RTG has pledged at least 18 billion baht guaranteeing free education for all local students till the age of fifteen as well. The RTG is also attempting to plug the estimated shortfall in demand of 100,000 teachers by waiving the normal entrance test (to become civil servants) for new recruits, so the government is clearly doing a lot to improve things and making Thailand a more attractive place to teach and study.

Other examples abound e.g. the company Corporate English Consulting in the business English sector which is the first and only provider of the internationally recognized Business Language Testing Service (BULATS) test as part of the most widely accepted platforms for assessing English language teaching, the Common European Framework (CEF). This system is already the accepted benchmark for testing in business in Europe and is also being used in other lesser known places like the Kingdom of Saudia Arabia.

But perhaps the best example of a sign of the maturing of the Thai language teaching sector is the work that has been done by John Quinn at SEE TEFL in Chiang Mai. I say this because their teacher training centre has recently received full ISO 9001:2008 status as an educational provider which has to rank as a pretty significant "first" among the others in Thailand. It also provides a welcome choice for those who don't want to go down the traditional CELTA or Trinity teacher training route.

For those not familiar with this, ISO 9001:2008 is the latest version of the ISO standard for quality management systems. To gain this status, there is both internal and external auditing, and it is ISO that provides that external auditing. The standard includes elements like quality policy, which must be understood at all levels of the organization, quality decisions, quality management record-keeping, planning, and development, quality management, a regular performance review of internal auditing, and the precise documentation of procedures and exception management.

(The graduate trainees of the recent course, August 31st - September 25th, 2009, reproduced here by kind permission of SEE TEFL

All in all, this is a pretty comprehensive commitment for any organization to undertake, not to mention expensive, although the training costs at SEE TEFL were subsidised 50% by the Thai Ministry of Industry's SME centre in Chiang Mai.

What this in effect means is that SEE TEFL is certified and audited by Bureau Veritas. If you do a quick search on Google, it will tell you that this company is the world's leading certification body with over 80,000 clients in more than 100 countries, and a global network of 5,700 highly qualified auditors and expertise that is recognized by more than 35 national and international accreditation bodies. Pretty impressive indeed.

The SEE TEFL certification is accredited by the United Kingdom Accreditation Service (UKAS) which is the sole national accreditation body recognized by the UK government to assess, against internationally agreed standards, organizations that provide certification services.

I caught up with John recently and asked him about the success of his program and what he thinks of the maturing of the Thai EFL sector.

"The TEFL industry is still growing quite a bit and so it is best characterized as uneven levels of maturation. The fact that we have sought and been awarded this certification is one sign of increasing maturity, as with increasing competition the need to stand out and to set a standard and lead becomes more and more important."

I was keen to know more about this course as it is clearly growing in popularity. I asked a recent graduate, Peter Kenny, what he thought made the course special for him? He identified three main areas which are: price, the range of classes (taught in the teaching practice sessions), and the cultural awareness training.

"The main difference for a prospective student is that the cost is low but the quality is still good. The best thing was the range of classes that we prepared for: from college nurses to elementary school students. It was fun learning the Thai, and the cultural awareness was interesting."

Clearly, there are lots of positive things going on at SEE TEFL. I asked John about his future plans and where he sees his organisation in the next 5 years.

"We feel that we have set the standard for others to follow. We would like to encourage all course providers to be externally audited by professional independent organizations such as Bureau Veritas and follow quality standards recognized by an authority such as ISO. Currently we are considering an offer to open a second school in Asia. We will ensure first that quality is standardized wherever the SEE TEFL brand is used."

Something tells me there's a bright future ahead, not just for SEE TEFL, but for the Thailand education sector as a whole.

Reaching a TurningPoint

A form of classroom audience response software

2nd November 2009

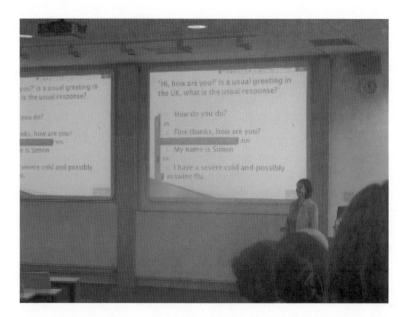

(Joanne Hooker, the Deputy Director of the Business and Management pre-sessional English course at the University of Birmingham, the UK, leads an end of course quiz using TurningPoint in September, 2009).

With so much educational technology in the classrooms these days, I decided this month to look at a form of classroom audience response software called TurningPoint which started its classroom life in America.

Einstein famously said that "the only thing interfering with my learning is my education". In other words, sometimes traditional forms of education don't work either because they can't cater for hidden geniuses, or because they simply fail to get all the students engaged in the dynamics of the lesson.

I'm sure that every teacher reading this will be able to think of at least one time when they looked over at their charges and felt a sense of unease, maybe even despair, at not being able to get through to them. I remember once when I was an undergraduate being in a seminar supposedly discussing a lecture on Dickens, and the room fell deadly silent only for the teacher to say that getting answers and comments from us was "like pulling teeth".

Well, now there's an answer of sorts to this dilemma - let's call it the "pulling teeth" syndrome because the new technology called TurningPoint has a much greater ability to get students talking and discussing aspects of the lesson content. In fact two American studies have shown that the interactive software can increase scores by as much as 15% between pre-testing and post-testing which is pretty impressive. Moreover, study after study has shown that the students themselves really enjoy TurningPoint classes and the feedback, often above 90%, has been that the vast majority of students were in agreement that if the clickers (explained below) were implemented in all classes, grades would improve. There are many other benefits, too, which I'll explain below.

How it works

TurningPoint is basically an extension of PowerPoint, so if you're already au fait and competent with one, the other is child's play in terms of getting used to its functions. Assuming all the equipment is available - a computer, the licensed software installed, one handheld wireless device per student called a "clicker", a large whiteboard or screen - you're ready to go. One point I want to stress right at the start is that the software works best with larger classes as it enables everyone to get involved and avoids the anonymity factor that inevitably comes about in larger groups.

Let's say you want to use it in a language class to review a grammar point e.g. the differences between present perfect and past simple. To begin with, you might want to review the form so could set a question like the following:

Which is the correct form of the present perfect?

1. Verb to be + verb 2

2. Verb to be + verb 3

3. Has/have + verb 2

4. Has/have + verb 3

Once you have polled this question, on your screen, and given the students a few seconds to select the correct answer using their clickers, you will see how many students have got it wrong or right as it is represented in graph or pie chart form on the whiteboard. (Incidentally, this is always useful for review purposes later e.g. for test preparation as you the teacher now know who has got the answer right or wrong!)

Next, you might decide to ask another question e.g. to ascertain the actual use:

When is the present perfect normally used?

1. To talk about actions happening now?

2. To talk about actions that happened in the past?

3. To talk about actions that will happen in the near future?

4. To talk about actions that happened in the past with a result in the present?

Of course, here we would only be concentrating on one usage and ignoring others e.g. present perfect for experiences, but another question can always be added to ascertain this. However, the real beauty of this software is that at every stage of the class, the students are engaged. As a follow up, and if you wanted to get a discussion going, you could present a question, poll the answers, and then easily split up the class into smaller groups, and give them 10 minutes to discuss the topic and answers in smaller groups. The groups could be formed in accordance with the answers given to an initial question, or using some other criteria. In fact, the list is endless as to what strategies a teacher could employ to use the software.

Straight from the horse's mouth

As I mentioned at the start, the academic studies that have been done on this are extremely positive, but the people who have to use it themselves, the teachers, are really the ones to listen to in order to get a reasonably fair assessment of its worth in the classroom. I first saw a demonstration of this at the University of Birmingham this summer by Paul Foxall who gives demonstrations to other departments in the University. Here's what he had to say:

"One of the limitations of the traditional method of presenting is attention span of the passive learner. Studies have shown that the attention span of students falls off remarkably quick, maybe as soon as after 7 minutes! TurningPoint transforms a class into an interactive learning experience; stimulating peer discussion and peer instruction. A lecturer may ask a question and get a response from the class; the academic could then get the students to discuss their initial response amongst themselves, then poll the students a second time and compare and discuss changes in the feedback."

(Pupils using TurningPoint in a primary school in Pimlico, London, called Churchill Gardens Primary)

Mitt Nathwani is also a practitioner of the software. I asked him whether he thought it could be used successfully to teach a language?

"Yes but as part of a wider strategy of teaching. Nothing beats conversation and other traditional methods for teaching a language but TurningPoint can be used for example to check pupil' understanding of the rules of grammar in any language."

Mitt tells me that there are a number of different purposes to which the kit can be put. For example, it allows children to decide on the outcome of a story by voting, This is only done after first getting the children to write the story collaboratively and finishing it in their own words. Shakespeare can also be taught by analysing scenes and characters after first asking questions about what the pupils think of e.g. the characters, their traits and oddities, what dramatic devices are used by Shakespeare to bring his stories to life, and many other applications.

Likewise Ben Walsh, a teacher and historical author, agrees and suggests that teaching has advanced from the old "chalk and talk" days to a more collaborative style of learning.

"TurningPoint is very easy to use. Students simply press the appropriate key on the handsets to vote on what they think is the correct answer to the question I have given them. Being able to ask questions during the Challenge Day presentation helps to keep students more engaged in the lesson, and with the instant feedback I receive from their votes I can determine which issues they've understood and which we need to go over again. The students really like seeing the results to the questions and it makes the class more motivated rather than the more traditional ways of marking of class work."

If the numbers are anything to go by, TurningPoint is fast becoming a hot item in the UK as it has been for over 10 years in the USA. It's not easy to measure it in terms of actual users, but there around 190,000 handsets currently in the UK. Typically, educational establishments (schools, universities, colleges et al) are buying around 32 handsets each so you could say that there are 5,938 users. However, people normally share kits, so you could have, for example, four or five departments in a school sharing a kit. This means the short answer is probably several thousand users.

Personally, I think this software would be perfect for Thai classrooms which are often upwards of 40 students, sometimes more. I was once offered a job in a teachers' training college near Pinklao and told that (a) there were no set course materials and no curriculum, which meant I'd have to design my own from scratch, (b) that there was no additional money available for this, and (c) the absolute killer - there was a minimum of 50+ students in each of the three classes I was required to teach! One class had 66 students. For me this software is a welcome boost for teachers who are faced with large classes and boy do I wish I had that software back then! I'd be interested to know if anyone is using TurningPoint in Thailand right now or whether they think it is a good idea. What do you think? Send your answers and comments to - tomtuohy@hotmail.com

Teaching unions

Why isn't there protection for foreign teachers in the form of teaching?

1st October 2009

When you've stopped laughing for a minute, and wiped the tears from your eyes, you might want to consider why this question isn't so funny after all? Of course, I understand why people might think it's such a funny thing to actually believe that you could have some form of protection as a teacher in this country, but I don't see why it can't be achieved given some goodwill on both sides. The fact is that, as we all know, there isn't any form of protection at all for professional workers here never mind the teaching sector. In effect, in Thailand you are expected to take it or leave it when things don't go the way you expect them to.

Now, don't start thinking I am Lech Walesa, Jimmy Hoffa, or Arthur Scargill in disguise as I have only ever been in a union once in my life, and it was only for a few months, so I'm not what you could ever safely call a "union" man. I just happen to think there are a lot of benefits for organizations on both sides of the fence to get together and work out differences around a table like mature adults. Better that than the current philosophy which is - if you are not happy with the status quo in Thailand, you need to "take a hike" because if you find yourself being exploited by unscrupulous teaching agencies, refused payment from employers, or just simply treated as a vehicle for making money by owners of schools, there isn't a thing you can do about it.

When things go wrong...

When things go wrong, and they invariably do in any organisation where employees and employers reside without any form of arbitration, whom do you turn to for help? Who can negotiate for you and help you to 'walk the walk' and tread the fine line between demanding your rights and avoiding insulting your hosts? When a school has reneged on a promise to pay you a bonus, or when a promised holiday doesn't materialize, or when you are let go at a minute's notice, what can you actually do about it?

While I am not suggesting that all teachers here are in desperate need of protection, I am suggesting that they might, during their stay here, need some form of representation which is a right enjoyed in more developed countries. We all hear stories every day of the way teachers are sometimes mistreated and who have little invested in their professional development. They are usually told that this is the way things are done in Thailand and it's largely futile to complain.

This is especially true of new teachers who are often worked into the ground so that language school owners can maximize their profits while they have the teacher contracted to work in their school. When I first came here some thirteen years ago, I was expected to work six days a week for 23,000 baht. That typically meant some 30+ hours of classroom time every week. I would often be put under pressure to do extra classes on Sundays as well, which I sometimes did so that a 40-hour working week was not all that unusual (55-60 hours if you include preparation time). Of course, this is good in some ways because new teachers by definition are greenhorns and so the class time is invaluable in both building up a repertoire of skills and also instilling confidence in the teacher, too.

Speaking your mind

There is a reason I brought up this topic now. Doing research for an article, for The Guardian Weekly newspaper recently, I came across the recent brouhaha surrounding the Thai Culture courses in Thailand and saw an online petition on a local website. As a result, I asked a group of its members to give me a quote about their opinions. While giving honest opinions about their experiences through the secrecy that an avatar brings online, when it came to voicing their opinions publicly, not one person wanted to come forward to say something positive or negative about the teaching license.

This lack of speech speaks volumes. It says first and foremost that a lot of teachers here are afraid to speak their minds for fear of reprisals e.g. if their identity becomes known, they may not have their work permits renewed especially as it is actually an official law that if you show Thailand in a negative light, whether Thai or farang, you can be prosecuted. I also emailed the head of a very powerful organisation, which oversees the Thai Teaching Licenses without reply so it is not only westerners who feel this pressure to keep quiet

When I tried to get a quote from some veteran TEFL trainers, I didn't fare much better so there's clearly a problem here with those involved in the local education industry not having any kind of platform in which to air their views in an open, honest and therefore healthy way. Call me crazy but I happen to believe that when problems are not addressed early on e.g. on or around the time they happen, they tend to come along later and bite you in the butt twice as hard.

Current options...

Of course, there are arenas in which problems can be aired in Thailand. Dr. Timothy Cornwall, a fellow scribbler in The Bangkok Post's Education section, along with Ajarn Terry Clayton, head the Thailand Educational Network, (TEN) -http://www.thaiednet.org/dr-tim-cornwall.html which "...organizes a monthly opportunity for educators in Thailand to meet on a regular basis in a comfortable environment to share teaching and living experiences with colleagues and peers." Similarly, there are others like The International Schools Association of Thailand (ISAT), - http://www.isat.or.th/about_isat.asp which has the following among its responsibilities, "In addition to disseminating information to its members on educational information to its members on educational issues both at home and overseas, its regular meeting provide a forum for discussion, debate and the exchange of views and information."

There are others but the point I'm trying to make is that there isn't any one, overarching institution that is set up to take care of the high volume of teachers here like the National Union of Teachers in the UK, and this is especially important with the major reform that is currently taking place in the Thai educational system and the recent figures suggesting that between 1-1.5 billion people are learning English globally. If Thailand really is serious about reforming and modernizing its education system thereby taking the county into the next century, can it really afford not to have a system for dealing with the many problems - cultural, economic, practical that so many western teachers face in the country on a daily, basis?

What I'd like to see as teaching representatives are similar to the western style volunteer policemen that patrol Walking Street in Pattaya and who solve minor problems before they become major ones. Unlike the Pattaya guys and girls who do a fabulous job, the reps I'm talking about for the educations sector would be retired teachers, ex-school heads, inspectors, school administrators et al. Will that ever happen in Thailand I wonder? What do you think?

The dreaded teaching observation lesson

Angel or Daemon?

1st September 2009

We've all been in those sometimes terrifying situations when we are told that an observation is being scheduled. At that moment, reverberating in your ears, are those words that every teacher dreads - "teaching observation", and for a nanosecond, time seems to stop or at least get caught in some eternal loop like the space between two Venn diagrams.

It's then a mad scramble to pore through all your best lessons in an attempt to come up with something that resembles a professional, slick, lesson with all the bells and whistles of TEFL-dom; something that shows you know the inner dynamics of this arcane world of language learning; that you know your TTT from your PPP, and your L1 from your IELTS.

Having started my first official TEFL job thirteen years ago in a large private language school in Bangkok, which also doubled as a CELTA training centre, I consider myself lucky as I was observed by Trainee TEFLers on a regular basis for about two years, with the result that I can say with absolute truth that I was observed more times in those first two years than I have the total number of times in my teaching career since.

I would often have my lessons hacked apart by those trainees who were long on theory but short on practical experience. They had been taught the staple diet of TEFL Dos and Don'ts and were eager to cut their teeth on my lessons, so any overconfidence or vanity that might have developed in those early years was soon nipped in the bud by the sometimes scalding comments in that cauldron of a teaching environment, and I'm extremely thankful for it.

For this reason, I am not one of those faint-hearted, wallflower-like TEFLers who shudder at the thought that someone will be coming to my classroom to stare up at me in a schoolmasterly way, with pince-nez glasses, write down every syllable of every instruction bleated out, then tear apart my lesson plan and expose me as a fraud! Yet this feeling persists, and there are many out there who avoid observations as though they were some form of cat and mouse detective game like the one played by the detective Porphyry and Razkalnikov in Dostoevsky's *Crime and Punishment*.

The Purpose

What therefore is the purpose of an Observation lesson? Ideally it should be to evaluate the teaching skills of a teacher which includes their classroom management techniques, specific delivery methods, monitoring skills, concept checking, presentation skills, and the entire gamut of a typical language learning class.

When I did my 6 hours of teaching practice at Stoke-on-Trent College many moons ago, I received really positive and useful feedback about my teaching style which somehow moulded me and, without foisting a particular style upon me, allowed me to make mistakes in a relatively stress free environment. This left me free to develop my own approach to language teaching and at my own pace through trial and error. When I got it wrong, I learned from it. When something worked, I learned from that, too.

In many ways, doing the CELTA is like taking your driving test. You learn all the rules like Mirror, Signal, Manoeuvre, and how to understand the Thinking, Braking, and Overall Stopping distance dynamic, but as soon as you pass the test, you start breaking all the rules and cross your arms when moving the steering wheel, instead of holding it at ten-to-two or quarter-to-three like your are supposed to. Does this make you a worse driver? In the same way, does not following all the formal rules of pedagogy make you a lesser teacher? Answers on a postcard to...

Around the world

While this may be what is expected from a teaching observation, it has rarely been the case in my experience of teaching in places like Japan, The Kingdom of Saudia Arabia, and Thailand. In Thailand for example, other than the first two years mentioned above, I was only observed approximately four times in the following years and two of those were demonstration lessons for job applications. In fact the quality and quantity of observations has varied wildly throughout my teaching career.

In the Thai university where I worked for close to five years, and which also had an international English program, I was observed only once, and that probably doesn't even count as an observation, as my boss, a Thai manager, slipped unannounced into my class one wet Wednesday afternoon for about twenty minutes, then disappeared. No follow up feedback was offered and, in fact, the entire episode was never mentioned again. This led me to believe that the observation was more about him being able to tick a box on some management form or, just as much a waste of time, to let me know who was boss rather than being designed for me to gain any pedagogical benefit from it.

In The Kingdom of Saudia Arabia, things were not much different. When I worked in a military establishment, I was observed three times in three months by a non native speaking Arab who was minus a CELTA or any form of TEFL certification, but who criticized me for giving out vocabulary sheets during the observation even though they were dispensed by company employees from the Teaching Supplies store room-cum-supplementary materials' area.

During my final observation, the Arab observer and three full colonels walked around my classroom often blocking the cadets' view of the whiteboard in a classroom where the air conditioning was not functioning and, at one point, it looked as if at least two of my sleep deprived cadets were going to pass out. This for me was another instance of the questionable value of teaching observations as it was more akin to a power game than intended to make me a better teacher.

Reality check

The fact is that observations vary wildly depending on where you go, and it begs the question as to what their real value is? After all, you wouldn't ask a doctor to give a demonstration on how he uses his stethoscope before a physical examination, or ask a plumber to demonstrate his use of a wrench before fixing your leaky pipe, so why should you expect an experienced language teacher to demonstrate their knowledge of the present perfect continuous, or explain how they will teach minimal pairs? If they come with good references and, in an interview, can answer questions on classroom management, grammar, and pedagogy, shouldn't that suffice?

This suggests that, in the fast paced language teaching world where time is often at a premium, teacher development becomes a side issue, which often gets forgotten about, and so the teaching observation is primarily used as an instrument for checking what's going on in the classroom rather than for developing the skills of the teaching practitioner.

EFL Teaching in Thailand (and elsewhere) part two

What's the best and the worst class you've ever taught?

1st August 2009

As promised, here are some of the lighter moments that I have been privy to in my time as an ajarn in Thailand; a time that, give or take one or two visits elsewhere, has lasted about twelve years. To be honest, I don't have to think that hard to come up with memories of my good classes as they spring to mind with relative ease.

Me Tarzan, you...

One such is a class I taught when I was at the ECC branch mentioned in my previous column. This was a 3-hour Sunday morning class I had for over a year, and it mostly consisted of single or divorced women between the ages of about 28 to 50 years old. In they would trundle every Sunday without fail and plonk down an assortment of fruit, nuts, Chinese kanom, odd nick-nacks, and anything else they thought I might like. It was as if they were trying to outbid for me in some weird car boot sale except there were no unwanted items, and the only thing that seemed to be on sale was me!

Had anyone chanced to stick their head around the classroom door, they could have been forgiven for thinking that I was some visiting chief at a tribal ceremony for my teacher's desk resembled one of them scenes from a "Carry on Up the Jungle" movies where the characters all visit a distant tribal king in a faraway African village and, as a peace offering or bribe, bring along everything that isn't nailed down on the way.

Of course, most western teachers will be familiar with this scenario - the young ajarn farang who has the women hanging on his every syllable because he is perceived as (a) single, (b) approachable, and (c) has all the accoutrements of western-ness aka white skin, blue or green eyes, etc., etc.

Being only in my early thirties, I was also very nubile in their eyes - in other words "marriageable" like that famous line from Charlotte Bronte's book - "It is a truth universally acknowledged, that a single man in possession of a good fortune must be in want of a wife".

There was Noy who was a 40-something stock market trader for a finance firm (sadly I believe one of the 50 finance firms or so that went under in the crash of 1997). She would sidle up to me and, within a hair's breath, ask what I was doing that evening and whether I'd like to go to a party or visit some rich relative in Ayutthaya. No matter how many times I knocked her back, she would come in again the next week with the same Bambi like eyes and the same optimistic smile which nothing seemed capable of diminishing.

Another was Oey who had her own way of press ganging me into romantic submission. One time after class, when all had said their goodbyes, she decided to be a bit more daring and, when I had turned around from cleaning the whiteboard, she, after unbuttoning the top part of her blouse, had installed her face on the edge of my nose. For a moment, I didn't know what to do or where to look, but she had it all rehearsed: "You lonely? Want girlfriend? I lonely too! We lonely together be ok nah?"
How could I fault her logic?!

No Introductions necessary...

For me, one of the funniest experiences I have ever had in a classroom was when I was a teacher in a relatively new class of students. I believe it was only the second or third class of this particular course. There I was at the start of the class waxing lyrical about something like homework or some such thing, and in walks this stunning young lady called Kok (yes, a bit of a mismatch, but Thais do like to give themselves unusual nicknames!) and sits down. As she is new, I ask her to introduce herself to everybody. She is a bit nervous, so I try to help by introducing myself and the other students first. Eventually, and somewhat hesitantly, she offers the following:

'Hello, my name is Supaporn, but you can give me Kok'.

Ok, I gingerly reply,

'Nice to meet you Kok'. So, tell us a little bit about you. For example, what do you want to do when you graduate?'

Quick as a flash she replies,

'Sir, I would like to be an air hostage!'

Speckles of laughter descend on the room. I try to regain some sense of order and try to rescue Kok.

'So, tell us Kok, this sounds like an exciting job. What would you have to do in this job?'

With an angelic smile on her face that could have made you think she was Florence Nightingale's daughter, she replies,

'I would have to service the passengers sir.'

Don't you want me baby...?

But if you think that mishaps with the Thai language can only happen to Thais, you'd be wrong. The following is an experience I had when I had not been in Thailand all that long. I was working for a company on Wireless Road in the heart of Bangkok. I had gone to the bathroom to take a leak, and when I returned someone had put a note on my desk asking me to go and see a Thai member of staff. Curious, and wanting to practice my limited Thai with her, I walked up to her desk and, in my best Thai, tried to say 'did you want me?' which I thought in Thai was the following:

'khun ow pom mai crap?'

She was in hysterics for five minutes, during which a crowd of more Thai staff had gathered around to see what was going on. When she managed to pull herself together, after almost being on the floor with laughter, she asked me to repeat it, so I did. Now the entire crowd was in hysterics. When they had all returned to normality, I asked them for the real translation of what I just said - 'Do you want (sexually) me?'

Showing interest...

Of course there are numerous examples of classes where I have had memorable time teaching my charges. I once had a kids' class at a well known kids' international English program which again lasted over a year. I had endless fun watching them interact with each other yet never was there any hint of the kind of jealous rivalry that would be a certainty in a farang kids' class such are the Thais so well behaved even at that age.

Another class was at The Bank of Thailand. The students were always on time, full of enthusiasm, did anything I asked of them and never once complained. They would always offer to take me to lunch, offer me snacks and fruit, offer me umbrellas when the rainy season came, and were a real delight to teach.

It was one of those classes were everyone got along and the atmosphere was really great. The class itself lasted a few months and consisted of mostly managers and senior staff which could often spell a disaster given that kind of dynamic (as I have experienced on many other occasions), but these were among the nicest students I ever taught, and I still get occasional emails from them to this day, some eight years after teaching them.

I remember this one from a student after a particularly long and difficult course where I had felt a complete failure in getting my message across to the students. On his way out the door, one student turned around and said, with complete sincerity and a big smile on his face, 'Goodbye. Come to see us when you are interesting!'

EFL teaching in Thailand

What's the best and the worst class you've ever taught?

1st July 2009

Go on admit it - we've all, at some point or other, been in situations in a classroom environment when we were close to losing it. I don't just mean having an off day when everything you did went pear-shaped, and try as you may, you just couldn't make any activity work.

No, I'm talking about times when you were within a hair's breath of strangling one or many of your charges: when acts of violence seemed only moments away and you had to pull every fibre of your being together in order to restrain yourself from doing something that would stop you from teaching ever again.

Equally, there have no doubt been times when you have actually looked forward to going to teach because the students were all a paragon of virtue, bringing you fruit and cakes, and other assorted gifts, and being as mellow as a deer. Such students are rare, but I have been fairly fortunate to have many classes where I can say, hand on heart, they were a joy to teach! This month I'm going to share a few of my horror moments, and next month a few of the lighter ones as well.

The horror, the horror

Having been teaching for more than twelve years in places like Japan, the UK, West Africa, Thailand and the Kingdom of Saudia Arabia, I guess you could say that I would have inevitably had a few moments when I was far   from   in   control.
I remember once when I hadn't been teaching long, I was about to go home when the Burmese manager of my school at ECC came up to me and asked if I could fill in for a colleague who'd just been told that his sister had been fatally injured, and that he had to return to Ireland for the funeral.

Thrusting a copy of Headway into my chest and a class register, he promptly started to march off somewhere else. Trying to seize the initiative, I had the presence of mind to ask him, "what time does the class start?" to which he replied, after checking his watch, "ten minutes ago". Up I hurried mentally trying to come up with a plan, what is often called in this business "door handle" planning.

When I arrived, I was greeted by about eight students who all looked at me with a mixture of dread and disgust. Still somewhat of a greenhorn, I should have seized the moment and exerted my authority right there and then, but didn't and was about to learn a very good lesson in classroom management.

Little did I know that these students worshipped the ground that my Irish colleague walked on, and that when I walked in, I could have been Mother Theresa, and it would not have mattered a jot. Also, I was not to know that this was the last class of a 40-hour course where the end-of-course test had been already completed, and the students were only there to have a party for the aforementioned teacher. This I should have guessed when I saw a few plastic cups and bottles of pop partially hidden under some of the chairs.

"Good afternoon" I said, "I'm your teacher for today", trying to sound authoritative. I didn't work. "Who can tell me where you all are in the book?" Silence. I looked around the room. "Ok, let's take the register" I said, trying to rescue things. More silence. When names were called, answers were offered somewhat begrudgingly, and soon the register was complete.
I decided to bite the bullet. "Ok, turn to chapter twelve. We are going to look at the present perfect continuous". More silence. This really was new territory for me, and I started to realise that every time I gave instructions, the other students' eyes would all gravitate to an older Poo Yai lady in the corner with expensive looking Rayban sunglasses.

Writing on the whiteboard the form of the present perfect continuous, I tried to elicit some examples from the students, but again nothing was offered. Remembering what I was once told by my PE teacher at school in London, namely that if I was in a difficult situation, perhaps cornered by a group, "always go for the biggest and strongest first" he had told me.

With that in mind, I turned to Mrs. Raybans and asked her to give me an example of the present perfect continuous, but she just sighed and shook here head. More silence. "Can anybody else help Jim?" (Mrs. Raybans). More silence. Not to be outdone, I wrote some examples on the whiteboard and again elicited some use for the present perfect continuous. More   silence. Finally, when the silence had become deafening, I decided to find out what the problem was. "Do you want to study today?" All eyes turn to Mrs. Raybans. The heads go down in a semi huddle, and some whispering in Thai ensues like those contestants from the University Challenge quiz show.

"No" says Mrs. Raybans quite pointedly.
"Ok, would you like another teacher?" More discussions.
"No" says Mrs. Raybans.
With little dignity left, all I could do was pick up my things and politely leave.
The following morning, I bump into the Burmese manager again and he has a big smile on his face.
"How was your fill-in class yesterday?" he asks.
"Not so good" I reply. "They didn't seem to want to study".
The Burmese manager laughs.
"You know the older lady? With the sunglasses?" he asks.
"Yes?"
"She says you 'shamed her with your eyes!'"

More like space cadets

On another occasion, I was in Saudia Arabia teaching a bunch of Royal Saudia Arabian Air Force cadets. As usual, they were completely knackered having run around the parade ground in the day, and from being woken up at all hours of the night to be brutalized by the Saudia officers.

In fact the hardest part about teaching these cadets was not that they were lacking in any discernible language skills, but in trying to get their attention when all they wanted to do was sleep. However, with officers walking past the classrooms every few minutes or so, they knew that this was not a viable option, and it was my job to give them a chit for punishment if they were disruptive or fell asleep.

On one occasion, two cadets fell asleep. I asked the cadets next to them to wake them up, but they wouldn't budge. I tried again, but anything I said fell on deaf ears, so having no choice, I went over to my desk and began to write out their names on the punishment chit.

Suddenly, one student wakes up, sees what I am doing and walks over to my desk in a threatening manner.
"What you do teacher?"
"I'm writing out a chit. You have been warned three times and now you will have to go and explain to the officers why you were sleeping."
Then the other cadet wakes up and walks over to my desk.
"Why you give me chit teacher?"
"Because you were sleeping."
"Yes, but why teacher?"
I explain again.
"Yes, but why teacher?" repeats the first cadet.

This goes on for another minute, like a Laurel and Hardy skit, and then feeling I have no other option or I'll lose control of the entire class, I give them an ultimatum.

"Either you both go to see the officer, or I will go there myself and explain that you refused to go!"
Some Arabic is exchanged and I can see that the first cadet is visibly angry. His face looks like Mt. Krakatoa before an eruption.
"Ok, I go to officer and tell him you said f**k **f".

Initially, I am shocked and am not sure that this is what he has actually said, so I ask him to repeat it. He does although it comes out as fack up (or something like it). A few gasps are evident from the less troublesome cadets and I now know for sure that this linguistically challenged cadet really has said what I thought he said. With little choice I pick up my things and go to see the officer. Half an hour later, I look out of the window and see both cadets standing alone in the parade ground, the temperature probably around 45 degrees C, and all I can see are two bodies swaying rhythmically in the Arabian sun.

Book him Danno, murder one...

On another occasion in the same classroom in Saudia Arabia, it was break time, and I was reading some course material. As usual, cadets were mingling in and out of the classrooms, as was their habit. One cadet came in and sat down in a cadet's chair adjacent to my desk. Largely ignoring him when he kept asking me my name and such like (a common occurrence), I carry on reading.

Next thing I know I feel a thud on the side of my face. The cadet has picked up one of my student's books and hurled it at me before fleeing from the classroom. Again the officer comes to the class, I explain, and that cadet is seen in the parade ground doing one-handed press ups in the hot sun.

During my time there, I had various items stolen including an expensive pen, had my teacher's bag rifled through many times, and witnessed a cadet deliberately sneeze all over a new teacher with the result that green snot was seen trickling down his shirt!

Boys will be boys

Once in Japan, I was required to teach a 7-year old called Keko who hated English almost as much as I hate those slimy, green things they put in Big Macs. The lesson always followed the same dynamic. In would walk the little monster, usually 5-10 minutes late, dragging his satchel on the floor, and a look on his face that would make a recent widow look happy.

When I asked him to get out his books and his pencil case, he would do so, but with the speed of a wounded sloth or some other incredibly slow-moving animal e.g. a panda bear. There were times when I thought he was in slow motion so slow were his movements. Then came the coup de grace: always the same without any deviation in timing or character.

Somehow, mysteriously, his pencil case would fall on the floor as if by magic, and he would get down on his knees to pick all the contents up. It didn't matter what I said or how I entreated him to pick them up quickly and put them on the desk, for he would sit there and, one by one, put each pencil, pen, crayon etc., into exactly the place designated for it in his pencil case! Then about ten minutes later, he would emerge from under the desk, a big smile beaming on his face, and the lesson proper would begin.

When I told the Japanese owner of the school, Mayumi, what happened, she quoted an English idiom back to me - "Boys will be boys. Isn't that what you say in your country?"

To queue or not to queue?

The changing nature of cultural norms in Thailand

1st June 2009

"**A** Nation of Shopkeepers" ("L'Angleterre est une nation de boutiquiers") is a disparaging remark supposedly used by Napoleon to describe the English. However, whilst Napoleon was referring to their unreadiness for war (the sense in which he meant it), most people remember that phrase as conferring a sense of cultural identity as somehow being "English." Thais also have their own sense of identity, something that marks them out and confers their own sense of "Thai-ness", although this is something that is changing faster than the CEOs of American banks.

If, like me, you have lived in the Kingdom for a number of years, you may have noticed a relatively new phenomenon. Certainly since the advent of the BTS, there have been a number of cultural changes that have taken place. One has been a noticeable trend by Thais to form orderly queues at bus stops, outside elevators, in government buildings, and at taxi ranks.

As that Aussie Croc Hunter would have said: "Crikey! What's going on mate?" The idea of queuing up for something was hitherto completely alien to a Thai, so what has happened to cause this sea change?

Influx of foreigners

Undoubtedly, the sheers volume of foreign visitors to Thailand over the years has been a major contributing factor. Since the Amazing Thailand tourism promotion campaign from 1998-1999, the numbers for tourist visitors has gone up dramatically, year on year. Indeed, according to Wikipedia, tourist numbers have grown from 336,000 foreign visitors and 54,000 R&R soldiers in 1967, to over 14 million international guests visiting Thailand in 2007.

What this means is that with such a high volume of people visiting these shores, with all their cultural as well as normal baggage, there was bound to be some repercussions, some changes in the way Thais behave. Some of this may be deemed good and, well, some bad, but either way, it shows a trend that is unlikely to abate.

Remembrance of things past ("À la recherche du temps perdu")

Back in 1997 when I first arrived here, there was no subway system and, of course, no BTS. What that meant was, if you were a chalky (teacher) like me, you invariably needed to supplement your meagre income by doing corporate teaching, unless, by some miracle of frugality, you were able to live on 23,000 baht a month.

This usually involved one or two of my own Proustian-like 'Madeline moments,' hopping on one of them old, red, non-air con buses, dashing through the Bangkok metropolis at breakneck speed. (Ok, I exaggerate - actually it was more like, sitting on one of them buses in sweltering heat, stuck in endless traffic, and me praying that the traffic lights would change so that the Mexican air conditioning would kick in e.g. air would enter through the open windows of the bus.)

Personal experience

On one such occasion, I had been on my way to teach at the Database Department at the Thai Docks on Rama IV Road. It was during the Hot Season and, when I disembarked from the bus, I'm sure I must have looked like a corpse recently dredged from the Chao Phraya. As usual, I headed for the nearest 7-11 to get a Coke and generally cool down in the welcome air con of the shop. Having formed a queue behind a young lady, I thought, in my very smug, British way, I was doing the right thing.

When it came to my turn to be served, a Thai man entered the shop and stepped in front of me to order some Krung Thep cigarettes. Unperturbed, I waited for the other assistant to offer me eye contact, but then a girl wafted a pack of Mama instant noodles in his face and, again, I was unable to pay for my drink. Feeling more than a bit disconsolate, I turned back to the original assistant who had unfortunately started to take money from another customer. In the end I walked out in disgust.

Of course this was the wrong reaction, as it hadn't really occurred to me back then (having only been in the Kingdom a short time) that Thais don't actually queue up for things, so I'm sure I learnt a valuable lesson that day.

On another occasion, not long after it had opened, I was on the BTS and was getting off at Siam Square readying myself to face the usual hordes of passengers waiting to get on. One woman in particular was hell-bent on getting on, but the only way for her to achieve her aim was for her to literally go through me. As there was nowhere for me to go (being surrounded by other passengers, I remembered Tennyson's Charge of the Light Brigade poem, "canons to the left, canons to the right...) I continued pushing forward in order to get off the train. Instead of stepping to one side, which would have been the sensible thing to do, this lady tried to push me out of the way.

I am sure that, if you haven't seen the movie version of David and Goliath, you are probably familiar with the basic story. Try imagining a short, 40-kilogram, slightly built Asian woman barging into a large, 95-kilogram male and imagine the result. I'm ashamed to say the lady hit the floor like a proverbial 'sack of potatoes'. Embarrassed, I leant down to try to help her to her feet, but she got up by herself and gave me a look that I am unlikely to ever forget. It was something I interpreted as, 'crazy foreigner, you should learn how we do things here'. Fortunately, she wasn't hurt, but one wonders if she learnt something valuable that day? I hope so. I know I did.

Teaching discursive or creative writing

Why isn't creative writing taught in Thailand in general?

1st May 2009

At first glance this may seem like a silly questions, but why aren't there that many courses that teach the basics of creative forms of expression in writing in Thailand, instead of students simply being asked to regurgitate, often with parrot-like efficiency, the input from the teacher in the lesson using continually unchanging media? Surely, it can't just be because local educators feel that Thai students aren't up to the task for that would be a complete cop out, right?

I did a quick search on Google.com and came up with the following schools which do or have provided 'creative' writing modules in Thailand in the past: Ruam Rudee International School, Thammasat University, Mahidol University International College, Lanna International School, The American School of Bangkok, Australian International School Bangkok and the International School of Bangkok.

Whilst this list is not meant to be exhaustive, if you look long enough, you'll soon start to see a pattern develop. In other words, where "creative" writing programs are offered, they are usually at a high-end school such as those above, not in the Thai National Curriculum, and most definitely not at the lower end of the educational scale in Thailand e.g. in the temple schools or poorer Thai schools.

The traditional model

Most western teachers reading this will be familiar with the basic mainstay of EFL teaching e.g. Reading, Writing, Listening and Speaking. These subjects are traditionally taught using the three Ps: Presentation, Practice, Production - the standard TEFL methodology. EAL, ESOL, EAP, TPR,

219

and other teaching methods have their own working dynamics, but often incorporate some or all of this approach, too.

Within each of these subjects is a variety of ways of developing skills to get the message across, and the learning outcome achieved, so for example, in Reading, a student learns strategies such as skimming and scanning, understanding paraphrasing, summarising, and various lexical sets of vocabulary etc., etc. Listening too will have its own sets of approaches, such as, pre-listening activities, listening to CDs, note taking skills, and so on.

Likewise, Writing has a fixed way of being taught in general which usually involves the teacher setting up an assignment with clear objectives, and the student being required to produce a completed written text of varying lengths, whether as a controlled activity or a freer based one. However, what's noticeable about typical Writing courses, certainly where Thailand is concerned, is that they rarely ever deviate from what could be called the standard 'norm' or regular practice, as the output is always related to something outside of the student.

For example, if the writing task is a Geography assignment: writing about the evolution of an earthquake, or in Literature: writing about the meaning of a Shakespearean sonnet, the student is merely required to react to the media e.g. give a written opinion or evaluation of it, not be proactive - not create an original medium themselves.

In the world of EFL, the task might be to write about a story or set of facts presented using a CD or a reading text, but it would always be based on the story as listened to or read, not a story that came from the student's own life experience. Why is this so?

Defining creative writing

By creative writing, I don't just mean the very narrow definition of 'storytelling' with characters, plots, and dialogue, though in my humble opinion, these are equally valid mediums for a language-learning classroom. What I mean is a much broader definition e.g. journalism, poetry, personal narratives, short stories, family histories, indeed the whole gamut discursive writing has to offer.

A lot of my own teaching experience (certainly related to the teaching of Writing) has only ever been in a middle ranking Thai university and a couple of private language schools, or when teaching Business Writing, although I can safely say that in my twelve years here in the Kingdom, I have rarely ever heard about any Thai schools that offer such a program, which should tell you a lot.

The fact is that the high-end schools know the value of such programs, yet it's still not clear why they are more likely to offer them when there really isn't that much extra to consider by way of additional cost?

Given all that's needed is to hire an industry qualified professional in accepted writing practices, someone with a reasonable amount of experience, it obviously must be for another reason, so why don't we see more of these types of programs?

So, again, I repeat my original questions - Why isn't creative writing taught in Thailand in general?

Advantages

There is a huge number of advantages, a few of which I'll list a few here. When you teach a child how to write a sentence or paragraph, using input from his or her own life, there is a sudden and dramatic interest in the child's level of interest because now, that child has something invested in his or her education. They are not simply learning by rote e.g. a process paragraph on how to write about the dynamics of photosynthesis in a Biology class, or how to calculate the time difference between Sydney and Chiang Mai in a Geography class. Here they are invited to write about the world around them in a way that automatically necessitates that they include their own views and place within it.

It also encourages them to reflect on different techniques that strengthen their writing: the use of appropriate words to provide the required register, the targeting of sentences and meaning to reach different audiences, the use of figurative language e.g. metaphors, similes, idioms etc., etc., and the effect that has when used instead of more literal forms.

One of my earliest experiences of creative writing was in a classroom in the UK when I was about eleven. The teacher asked us all to create a story using only our imagination. I wrote a story about the God Thor from Norse Mythology who drove a truck and beat up bad guys. However, what was so memorable to me about this is it opened my eyes to the power of language and how I, a small child, could create something literally out of the thoughts in my head. It brought home to me the complete power of language. I was hooked. A writer was born.

Success Stories

One of the creative writing programs I took a look at when researching this is the program at Lanna International School, which I have to say, looks really great. Here are a few more advantages creative writing brings courtesy of their own website:

> Statement of Purpose: The course is designed to be studied by students wishing to extend their creative use of the English language. Students following this course will learn to:
>
> > • enjoy the experience of writing without being penalised for mistakes in usage;
> > • understand the structure of different types of writing;
> > • demonstrate ability to communicate stories, thoughts, and experiences through writing;
> > • appreciate different ways in which writers achieve their effects;
> > • see writing as a means of social action in areas of human concern;
> > • enjoy and appreciate variety of language;
> > • understand themselves and others better through writing;
> > • free themselves of writer's block through creative activity;
> > • prepare a portfolio of publishable-quality writing;
> > • originate and/or edit school paper articles.

(http://www.lannaist.ac.th/ Reproduced here by kind permission of the Headmaster of Lanna International School, Mr. Roy Lewis.)

You don't have to be a genius to see that there are a lot of advantages in encouraging students to be more creative and expressive in their writing. Lanna International School produced three recent winners out of the five awards in a Dublin based competition to find winners of the 4th Junior

IMPAC Dublin Literary Awards for Thailand, Northern region. The winners were announced in a ceremony held on January 11th, 2009, at Citylife Magazine - the regional coordinator for the contest. The essay-writing contest was open to Thai students aged 14-18, writing in English on the topic "If We Could Change the World."

Conclusion

Instead of simply putting your kid into a regular school which will provide him or her with a sound basis in the Three Rs, step back and think a bit more about what other opportunities are open to your child to make him or her a more rounded individual.

If you want him to know what the present perfect tense is, her how to score well on an IELTS test, or how either can say hello to English-speaking guests to your home, then put him or her into a traditional school where they'll be fine.

However, if you also want your child to be able to give his opinion about a current topic in the news, or her to be able to tell a story using well-known narrative elements, then enroll your child in a school that will provide all the necessary language skills, so that, throughout his or her life, your child will always be able to communicate in a much more creative way.

Complete list of works cited

Books:

An Introduction to Language, First Canadian Edition, (1997), Harcourt Brace, Canada

Baldassare, Castiglione, *Book of the Courtier,* translated by Leonard Eckstein Opdycke, published by Courier Dover Publications, (2003)

Bryson, Bill, *Mother Tongue*, Penguin Books, (1991)

Coleridge, Samuel Taylor, *The Rime of the Ancient Mariner*, published by: Dover Publications Inc. paperback 28 February, (1971) - text of the 1798 version. http://en.wikipedia.org/wiki/The_Rime_of_the_Ancient_Mariner

His Holiness The Dalai Lama, *Ethics For The New Millennium*, Howard C. Cutler, M.D., Putnam Publishing Paperback, May 2001

Eliot, T. S., *The Wasteland and Other Poems*, Barnes & Noble Classics Series, (2005)

Holmes, Henry and Tangtongtavy, Suchada, *Working with the Thais,* White Lotus Co., Limited, (1995).

Triandis, Harry C., *Individualism versus Collectivism*, Westview Press, (1995).

Wittgenstein, Ludvig, *Tractatus Logico Philosophicus*, 6.1, Routledge Classics, Second edition (September 1, 2001)

Website articles:

Bob, Bangkok, *Bangkok Transport, Getting Around Bangkok*, http://www.bangkokbob.net/transport.htm

Customs & Etiquette: When in Thailand - http://www.eslmonkeys.com/

Cafarella, Jane, *Thai Diary: Digging Beneath the Surface* - http://www.abc.net.au/rn/talks/lm/stories/s1304563.htm

Caveman, *A Caveman's Point Of View Of The Thai Economy*, http://www.stickmanbangkok.com/reader/reader209.html

Cleary, Stephen, *Do's & Don'ts....To Truly Unseen Thailand*, http://www.thai-blogs.com/

(Editorial) *Funny Language*, http://www.chiangmai-chiangrai.com/funny_language.html

Fraser, Daniel, '*Thai Smiles - Good, Bad, Ugly, and the 10 in between*'. http://www.smilingalbino.com/stories/smiles.as

Gotthelf, Kristian, *The Asian Women's Shopping Experience: New research from Thailand*, June 20, (2003) http://www.asiamarketresearch.com/news/000309.htm

(Editorial) Mother Goose, *Peter Piper picked a peck of pickled peppers* http://www.amherst.edu/~rjyanco94/literature/mothergoose/rhymes/peterpiperpickedapeckofpickledpeppers.html

Niratpattanasai, Kriengsak *Expatriate Perceptions of Thai Colleagues* - Survey Results http://www.apmforum.com/columns/thai45.htm

Pricewaterhouse Coopers, Thailand Retail Trade Figures, in *From Beijing to Budapest: New Retail & Consumer Growth Dynamics in Transitional Economies*, http://www.pwc.com/extweb/pwcpublications.nsf/docid/8fea5f592d0a712c80256f1c00547442

Roeland, Philip, *A bit of culture (1)*, http://www.ajarn.com/Contris/philiproelandjuly2005.htm

Seaberg, Michael P, (aka Cent The Central Scrutinizer), *Chok Dee For You And Me*, & Stickman's guide to Bangkok, Readers' Submissions - www.stickmanbangkok.com/Reader/reader1150.html

Suriyakham, Sippakon, *Bangkok shopping bargains*, http://www.smarttravelasia.com/bangkokshop.htm

Tarver, Nick, *What hope for a superficial education system?* http://www.ajarn.com/Contris/exwriters/nicktarvernovember2005.htm

(Editorial) *Thai teens get serious: New market research on the Thailand youth market*, http://www.asiamarketresearch.com/news/000258.htm

(Editorial) *Thailand Has World's Longest Place Name*
http://www.fun-with-words.com/longest_place_names.html

Wilde, Bob, *The Thai Smile*, http://www.ethailand.com/index.php?id=768

www.wellofwisdom.com/albert-einstein/0/quotes-author.html

Academic articles:

Embree, John F, *Thailand A Loosely Structured Social System*, American
Anthropologist, April-June, (1950) Vol.52 (2):181-193.
http://www.publicanthropology.org/Archive/Aa1950.htm

Knutson, Thomas J., *TALES OF THAILAND, LESSONS FROM THE
LAND OF SMILE*,
http://www.fulbrightthai.org/knowledge/read.asp?id=27&type=culture

Komin, Suntaree, *Psychology of the Thai People: Values and Behavioral
Patterns* (1990) in *NATIONAL CHARACTER IN THE THAI NINE
VALUES ORIENTATIONS*.
Kanjanapanyakom, Rachavarn, and Prpic, J. Kaya, *The Impact of Cultural
Values and Norms on Higher Education in Thailand*, Monash University,
Melbourne, Australia, Kasetsart University, Bangkok, Thailand (1997)

Landon, K., *Siam in Transition*, Chicago, (1939).
http://www.publicanthropology.org/Archive/

McHugh, Charles, *Reaction Profiles by Americans, Chinese, Japanese,
Thai, and Vietnamese on 'Skeletons in the Family Closet'*, Setsunan
University, Osaka, Japan.

Morris, Desmond, *The Human Animal: A Personal View of the Human
Species —The Language of the Body*, Journal of Linguistic Anthropology,
June 2003, Vol. 13, No. 1: pp. 123-124.

Siengthai, Sununta, *HR Practices in Southeast Asia*
http://www.asdu.ait.ac.th/faculty/FacultyByID.cfm?FacultyID=255

Thanasankit, Theerasak, and Corbitt, Brian, *Cultural Context and its Impact on Requirements Elicitation in Thailand*, EJISDC (2000) 1, 2, 1-19 The Electronic Journal on Information Systems in Developing Countries, http://www.ejisdc.org/ojs2/index.php/ejisdc/article/view/2

Ukosakul, Margaret, *'Face and Politeness in Thai Social Interaction'*, http://webhost.ua.ac.be/tisp/viewabstract.php?id=791

Newspapers & Magazines:

Coday, Dennis, *Fighting Corruption*, *NCR* staff writer, National Catholic Reporter
http://www.nationalcatholicreporter.org/todaystake/tt100803.htm

Fletcher, Matthew and Gearing, Julian, *'A School for Scandal? Politicians are accused of buying degrees'*, Asiaweek.com
http://www-cgi.cnn.com/ASIANOW/asiaweek/96/0719/nat5.html

Forestier, Katherine*, Hats off as Thais tread world stage*, South China Morning Post, Monday 11th April, 2005
http://www.classifiedpost.com/jsarticle.php?lcid=HK.EN&artid=3000010 622&arttype=CNEWS&artsection=CED&communitycode

Hemtasilpa, Sujintana, *Consuming With a Difference*
http://www.bangkokpost.net/ecoreviewye2004/retailing.html

Niratpattanasai, Kriengsak, *'Bridging the Gap, - Impressing the boss, alienating your colleagues'*, The Bangkok Post

Sharples, Jennifer, *Famous names have learnt to keep up the old school Thais*
http://www.telegraph.co.uk/global/main.jhtml?xml=/global/2003/03/17/ed schoo217.xml

Stoneham, Neil, The Bangkok Post, Learning Post, *THE INTERNATIONAL*

EDUCATION BOOM
http://www.bangkokpost.com/education/site2003/cvnv0403.htm

Editorials: *Making Thai History: 'A blow to school "tea money" heralds positive change'*, Asiaweek.com
http://www.asiaweek.com/asiaweek/magazine/2000/0512/edit2.html

Speeches:

Bonaparte, Napoleon, 'A Nation of Shopkeepers' ("L'Angleterre est une nation de boutiquiers") Origin unknown.

Churchill, Winston, in a speech as the British Home Secretary (1910

Churchill, Winston, remarks at a White House luncheon, June 26, (1954).

Roosevelt, Theodore, American president, speech in Chicago in April, (1903)

.

Further Reading

Additional websites:

http://www.thaivisa.com/forum/index.php?showtopic=10278&st=30

Assana Boocha day
http://www.sriwittayapaknam.ac.th/asanha.html

Makka Boocha Day
http://www.sriwittayapaknam.ac.th/makha.html

Merit Making
http://www.sriwittayapaknam.ac.th/images/tamboon/index.html

Lewis, *The Education Dilemna For The Little Ones*, Stickman's guide to Bangkok, Readers' Submissions, http://www.stickmanbangkok.com/reader/reader318.html

Stickman's guide to Bangkok, *THEY COST WHAT? I THOUGHT THIS WAS BANGKOK!* Stickman Weekly 6/7/2003 http://www.stickmanbangkok.com/Weekly/weekly113.html

Steve Cleary, *International Schools in Bangkok* http://bangkok.metblogs.com/archives/2005/08/international_s.phtml

Two-thirds of Thailand's schools 'in a coma' http://www.bangkokpost.com/News/23Aug2006_news03.php

Additional Books:

Turnbull, Sarah, *Almost French, Love and a New Life in Paris*, Gotham Books, (2002)

Fox, Kate, *Watching The English - The Hidden Rules of English Behaviour*, Hodder & Stoughton Paperbacks (2005)

Calvino, Italo, *Invisible Cities*, Vintage Classics, London (1997)

Camus, Albert, *The Outsider*, Everyman's Library, New York, (1993)

Index of Authors

About the Author

Tom Tuohy is married and lives in Bangkok, with his Thai wife. He has been a long-term resident of Bangkok having lived in the country for 15 years. He is a teacher by profession and a freelance journalist in his free time. He has written for the *English Language Gazette*, *jobs.ac.uk*, *The Guardian*, and *The Bangkok Post* among others. He is also currently working on his PhD Writing, looking into the role of outsiders in narratives and storytelling traditions. In his spare time, he likes to write fiction, play football, and to cook and eat Thai food.